Business, Politics, and Cigarettes

Multiple Levels, Multiple Agendas

Business, Politics, and Cigarettes

Multiple Levels, Multiple Agendas

Richard McGowan

Quorum Books
Westport, Connecticut • London

Library of Congress Cataloging-in-Publication Data

McGowan, Richard.
    Business, politics, and cigarettes : multiple levels, multiple
agendas / Richard McGowan.
        p.   cm.
    Includes bibliographical references and index.
    ISBN 0-89930-964-X
    1. Cigarette industry—Government policy—United States.
    2. Tobacco industry—Government policy—United States.   I. Title.
HD9149.C43U656   1995
338.4′767973′0973—dc20   95-7279

British Library Cataloguing in Publication Data is available.

Library of Congress Catalog Card Number: 95–7279
ISBN: 0-89930-964-X

First published in 1995

Quorum Books, 88 Post Road West, Westport, CT 06881
An imprint of Greenwood Publishing Group, Inc.

Printed in the United States of America

The paper used in this book complies with the
Permanent Paper Standard issued by the National
Information Standards Organization (Z39.48-1984).

10 9 8 7 6 5 4 3 2 1

Contents

Preface

The evolution of this book has taken many years. The general outline for the book follows that of my doctoral dissertation on the tobacco industry, which was completed in 1988. Obviously, there have been a great many developments that have had a dramatic impact on the cigarette/tobacco industry in the intervening seven years. These changes and the changes in my own thinking of how the business and public policy processes interact with one another had to be incorporated in the manuscript. Hence, this book has had a rather long gestation period (ten years!) but I hope it will give the reader a unique view of this immensely profitable but controversial industry.

There have been many studies (both books and articles) of the cigarette/tobacco industry. Therefore, any review of the literature on the cigarette industry is bound to be incomplete. What follows is certainly a very brief synopsis of this literature that should give the reader a sense of the variety of research on the cigarette industry. This research can be broken into three categories: economic studies, public policy studies, and business policy studies. The classic economic studies of the cigarette industry were conducted by Tennant and Nichols in the 1950s. These books focused on the structure of the cigarette industry as an oligopoly and the effect that this structure had on the pricing of cigarettes and on the suppliers of tobacco. This question is still debated even today. Economists (such as Harris, Becker, and Murphy) have also been fascinated with estimating the elasticity of demand for cigarettes, especially in trying to measure the effect that excise tax increases have had on cigarette sales.

With the coming of the smoking and health issue in the 1960s, economists turned their attention to measuring the effects of various public policy interventions on tobacco sales, such as advertising and smoking bans, as well as excise tax increases. The work of Tollison, Bass, Leu, and Hamilton typify this type of study and contributed greatly to our understanding of the effects that various actions taken by the federal government had on cigarette sales. Similarly, health care specialists also contributed their thoughts on the proper role public policy ought to play in discouraging cigarette smoking. Again, there have been many articles and books on this subject, with the work of Viscusi and Warner being a classic example.

As for the business policy that the cigarette industry developed in reaction to these various government interventions, there has been a great deal written on the "diversification" cigarette firms have undertaken during the past thirty years. Biggadike has studied this strategy extensively, but perhaps the classic work on this topic is Miles's *Coffin Nails and Corporate Strategies*, in which Miles elaborates in painstaking detail the manner in which the cigarette industry has used diversification as a survival strategy.

So why do we need another study of the cigarette industry? One simple reason is that the cigarette industry is constantly evolving and the changes that it undergoes seem to be prophetic in determining the relationships between government and other industries. This study will also differ from previous studies in these four areas:

1. This book will develop a model that seeks to explain the interrelationships between the business and public processes. Previous works on the cigarette industry have focused either on the business or public process but not on both simultaneously. By examining the interactions of both at once, one gets a much deeper appreciation of the complexity of the problems faced by policy makers in both government and business.

2. Previous studies have focused on the role the federal government played in regulating the cigarette industry. But in this latest round of regulation of the cigarette industry, the vast majority of the public policy initiatives have come from the state level of government. This has been a substantial change for the cigarette industry but it is one that is beginning to occur for many other industries throughout the United States, especially as they attempt to deal with environmental concerns. An empirical analysis of various public policy interventions on state sales will be conducted and should give the reader a much better understanding of the role of the state in determining the success or failure of public policy initiatives at the state level of government.

3. This book will also differ from previous business policy books on the cigarette industry in two respects. First, it will show how the diversification policy has developed from a "historical" perspective and will comment on the "success" of this policy. In particular, the book will present a case that the meaning of "success" for a diversification strategy has changed as the cigarette industry has

evolved. Second, there will be a detailed empirical analysis to see if the cigarette firms change their pricing polices in reaction to state cigarette excise tax increases.

4. Finally, there will be a unique study of how states formulate strategy for using the cigarette excise tax as a source of revenue. Two aspects will be analyzed. First, could states actually suffer from a reverse Laffer effect, that is, as cigarette excise tax rates are raised, could states suffer a loss in revenue? Second, do states compete with one another for cigarette excise tax revenues? This study ought to provide the reader with an interesting perspective of the many issues that public policy makers face when they try to determine an appropriate cigarette excise tax rate.

This study was made possible only through the efforts of many colleagues. First, I would like to thank Jim Post, who directed my doctoral dissertation on the cigarette industry at Boston University, especially for his patience in making me clarify my attempts to analyze the cigarette industry. John Mahon's enthusiasm and his sage suggestions for developing a theoretical model also played a significant part in the development of this book. My thoughts on the corporate business strategies of the cigarette firms have been refined by many discussions with Hassell McClellan, a colleague of mine at Boston College. I would also like to thank William Oszechowski of the Tobacco Institute for generously supplying me with data for this study although in no way has the Tobacco Institute influenced the results of this research. Although I am the same age as Nick Naylor, the protagonist in Christopher Buckley's *Thank You for Smoking*, luckily, I have no need to pay "for the mortgage." I would also be extremely remiss if I failed to thank Pearl Alberts, the Economics and Management librarian at Boston College. She has always been extremely helpful in providing me with data and pertinent articles on the cigarette industry.

Finally, I need to thank those people who have had to listen to me talk about the cigarette industry for these many long years. First, I want to express my gratitude to the many business policy and statistics students I have taught over the years. Their willingness to listen to my "war" stories has always encouraged me to continue my research in this troubled industry. I also need to thank the Jesuit communities at both Boston College and the University of Scranton as well as many of my Jesuit contemporaries who have had to endure many a long "dissertation" on my part concerning the trials and tribulations of the cigarette industry.

Of course, any deficiencies in the book can be attributed solely to me. I hope that the readers will be inspired to investigate further the various aspects and problems that make the cigarette industry such a fascinating and always timely subject for research.

Part I
The Cigarette Industry and Government

Introduction to the Cigarette–Government Controversy

Does the U.S. cigarette industry have a future?
Could *any* with so many enemies have a future?
How bullish can you get about a business whose customers are starting to look like pariahs?

Fortune, August 17, 1987, p. 70

These were the unpleasant questions that *Fortune* posed as it began a feature article on the embattled cigarette industry in 1987. Ironically, the same questions were being posed by *Business Week* seven years later in an article entitled "Tobacco: Does It Have A Future?" While many industries have had to face the first question of whether they have a future, few industries have been so profitable while facing that question! In 1993, the cigarette industry was the fifth most profitable one in the United States with operating profits of $5.2 billion on sales of approximately $15 billion. The two leading firms in the industry, Philip Morris and RJR Nabisco, have nearly 72 percent of the market (illustrating the industry's oligopolistic structure) and 80 percent of the profits (*Business Week*, 7/4/94, p. 25). While sales have declined during the past twenty years at the rate of .6 percent per year, operating profits have only declined twice during this period. While the declining sales figures are somewhat troublesome, the industry still claims that a little over 25 percent of American adults still have "the habit" (Tobacco Institute, *Facts about Cigarettes*, 1993). Certainly, the bottom line for this industry doesn't seem to indicate imminent demise. Yet many investors treat the stock of cigarette firms exactly in this manner. So, what is the threat?

The last two questions that *Fortune* posed provide the key to why the cigarette industry's future is so precarious. Indeed, this industry does have many enemies, and the issue that unites these various groups is the smoking and health issue. Cigarette smoking been linked with heart and lung disease and many forms of cancer. As a result, health organizations such as the American Cancer Society, the American Heart Association, and the American Lung Association, as well as many antismoking groups such as GASP (Groups Against Smoking Pollution), ASH (Action on Smoking and Health), and STAT (Stop Teenage Abuse of Tobacco), have made repeated appeals and attempts for more antismoking regulations and legislation.

In 1985, the smoking and health controversy entered a new phase with the advent of the "passive smoking issue." No longer could the cigarette industry claim that the harmful effects of smoking were confined to just the cigarette smoker. Evidence showed that people who inhaled smoke from the cigarettes of others suffered health effects too. Critics of the cigarette industry were now employing the phrase "rights of the nonsmoker." Armed with this additional ammunition that the passive smoking issue provided, antismoking groups such as GASP, ASH, and STAT are now no longer content with merely discouraging smoking but are campaigning to make cigarette smoking a socially unacceptable activity. In the spirit of this new antismoking campaign, the rhetoric of the antismoking groups has escalated to the point that they have labeled the industry's leaders as "murderers" (GASP *Newsletter*, January 1992). It would be fair to say that the aim of the critics of the cigarette industry is no longer merely to attack a vice but to destroy the cigarette industry.

To accomplish this goal, these critics have taken their case to every branch of government. The following list includes the type of actions that critics want a particular branch of government to enact. They include the following measures:

1. *Judicial*—filing numerous liability suits against cigarette manufacturers. The Cipollone decision accelerated this trend. (*Time*, 6/27/88, p. 48).

2. *Legislative*—initiating legislative proposals on both the federal and state level including:
   a. Bans on all cigarette advertising (federal)
   b. Bans on smoking in the workplace and government offices (primarily state)
   c. Increases in the excise taxes on cigarette (federal and state)

3. *Executive*—calls for this branch (again, at both the state and federal levels) to sponsor additional efforts to discourage smoking. The chief sponsors would be
   a. Surgeon General—the goal of having a "Smoke Free America" by the year 2000
   b. Health and Human Services (HHS)—additional funds for anti-smoking education programs
   c. State departments of health

While the driving force behind all of these measures is the smoking and health issue, the goals behind these various measures are sometimes quite different. These goals range from imposing financial liability on the cigarette industry (potential huge payments as a result of losing these liability suits) to discouraging smoking (excise taxes, smoking and advertising bans). These goals are not mutually exclusive but in fact can reinforce one another. If cigarette sales fall significantly, cigarette firms will be in serious financial difficulty. If cigarette firms face huge liability judgments, then they will be in no position to encourage sales. Some even have a dual purpose. For instance, the rhetoric supporting increases in the cigarette excise tax includes the need to raise revenue to balance the budget deficit as well as the need to discourage smoking (*Congressional Budget Office*, June 1993, p. 304).

What has made all of the recent antismoking activity unique has been the involvement of the state and local government in this issue. In 1980, there were 258 bills introduced at the state level and 31 bills at the local level to regulate smoking. In 1993, these figures increased to 806 at the state level and 324 at the local level (The Tobacco Institute, *The Tobacco Observer*, Spring 1993, p. 3). This is not to say that legislative activity is slowing down on the federal level. In 1993, the number of bills introduce to regulate cigarette smoking more than tripled from the number introduced since 1984 (ibid., p. 3).

Given that every branch and level of government seems to be interested in regulating it, the cigarette industry does indeed seem to be beset from all sides. Yet the industry also has political allies at every branch and level of government. At the national level, the congressional delegation from the "Six Tobacco States" (North Carolina, South Carolina, Kentucky, Tennessee, Virginia, and Maryland) and representatives from the Department of Agriculture have been protectors of the industry's interests. The industry has also formed a very effective lobbying network spearheaded by the Tobacco Institute, the industry's chief political representative.

The allies of the cigarette industry at the state and local level include various retail organizations, restaurant associations, and such diverse groups as the Advertising Council and the American Civil Liberties Union. The interest of these various groups in the smoking dilemma ranges from economic (advertising, retail) to philosophical and ethical (ACLU, Tobacco Institute).

But perhaps the most powerful argument the cigarette industry can muster against its numerous enemies is its economic contribution. In 1992, the core cigarette industries (for example, the growing of tobacco and the manufacture of cigarettes) employed over 400,000 workers and paid out almost $6.48 billion in compensation. Meanwhile, the supplier industries (for example, paper products and machinery) of the cigarette industry employed 296,000 workers and paid out almost $7.4 billion in compensation in 1993. Also, the cigarette industry, its suppliers, and its customers paid out over $20 billion in federal, state, and local taxes, with excise taxes accounting for over 60 percent ($11.9 billion) of these tax payments (Tobacco Institute, *The Tax Burden on Tobacco*, p. 1). Another interesting economic fact the cigarette industry has just revealed is that almost 5 percent of total U.S. exports are now tobacco related. It is obvious that the economic stakes of the cigarette industry are high indeed!

From the preceding discussion, it is apparent that the cigarette industry evokes an emotional response from many different factions in society. Some groups are demanding that government outlaw cigarettes or least discourage the use of cigarettes. Meanwhile, other groups see the cigarette industry as another business that has been interfered with by government, one that provides a very good livelihood for more than 1.59 million workers and whose "right" to existence should be left to the marketplace.

Yet in many ways the questions and issues surrounding the cigarette industry and the role of government in regulating it can be asked of any industry. What are the factors that cause government to interfere with the conduct of a business or an industry? What roles do the various branches and levels of government play in determining how an industry will be regulated? What measures should the government use to accomplish the goals that government has been given by society? How are the costs of the regulation measured? Are there any unintended effects of regulation? Who or what determines if the goals of regulation are being met? How does an industry respond to government actions directed toward it? What are the measures an industry can take to influence what course of actions a government will take?

The purpose of this book is to develop models and research methodologies that can be used to study the relationship between business policy and public policy. The cigarette industry will provide the basis not only for the models describing the relationship between business and government but also the sales data for testing the effects that governmental actions have had on cigarette sales.

The cigarette industry has had a stormy relationship with government throughout its history, and there are plenty of data to be analyzed. The models developed to study this industry and results from the analysis using these models can also be applied to analyze the stormy relationship between government and industries such as alcohol, drugs, and gambling.

The evolution of the cigarette industry is discussed in the next chapter. A short history of the cigarette industry will be presented, and it will be shown that the cigarette industry has undergone three waves of government regulation. The first two waves have been characterized by actions taken by the federal government whereas the third wave has seen the entrance of state and local government as regulators. This "wave" model will also underscore the point that with each succeeding wave, the pressure placed on the industry has increased in intensity and cumulative power.

In Chapter 3, a convergence model for business and public policy will be developed using the "Three Wave" model as its basic point of reference. This model will incorporate Freeman's stakeholder concept (1984) for describing the various groups that are interested in the public policy process and use Porter's model for illustrating the strategic groups involved in the business policy process. The unifying element of this model will be its "systems" connection as presented by Preston and Post (1975) in their "interpenetrating systems model." What is unique about this "Convergence Model" is its integration of stakeholder analysis, public policy analysis, and business policy analysis. Any model that hopes to provide a description of the relationship between the cigarette industry and the government has to be able to show not only how the various groups influence one another (stakeholder analysis) but also how the interests of various groups involved in the smoking issue change over time (public policy analysis) and the effects they have on industry (business policy analysis). The merger of these different types of analysis enables this convergence model to accommodate the various "stages" of development that the cigarette industry has undergone throughout its turbulent history.

Using the convergence model as the basis for viewing how the cigarette industry and government interact, Part II of the book will discuss the various hypotheses that can be drawn from this model. These hypotheses will test the effectiveness of the various regulations imposed by the government on the cigarette industry. The areas of greatest interest are the effect of government action on cigarette sales and on the pricing policies of the cigarette firms. The first set of hypotheses will test the effectiveness of the following measures on cigarette sales: the federal ban on cigarette advertising on TV and radio, public smoking bans, and various excise tax increases. A second series of hypotheses will examine the relationship between the pricing policy of the cigarette firms and the imposition of cigarette excise tax increases.

While many previous studies have examined these issues, two factors will make this study of these hypotheses unique. First, the cigarette sales data to be tested will be monthly for all fifty states from 1987 to 1994. Previous studies have had to use national data to draw conclusions about the effectiveness of various public policy measures. However, in the United States, because the cigarette excise tax rate differs from state to state, it is difficult to ascertain what exactly was the effect on cigarette sales when the measures were imposed.

The other unique feature of this research is the methodology used to test the time series data. Previous research on these questions used econometric models based on national data to determine the effects of various public policy measures on cigarette sales.

In this study, ARIMA (autoregressive integrated moving average) time series intervention analysis will be employed. There are two advantages to employing an ARIMA analysis instead of the more traditional econometric analysis. The first advantage revolves around the type and quantity of data. This data is seasonal, with two peak sale seasons, June (Father's Day) and December (Christmas). In general, sales tend to be higher during the late spring and summer months (June, July, August, and September) as will be shown in Chapters 4, 5, and 6. Hence, in order to fit any sort of multiple regression model, an unusually high number of dummy variables would be required, making the model very difficult to interpret. Since ARIMA analysis is specifically designed to handle long-term seasonal data (which this study happens to have), it is the appropriate time series methodology to employ.

There is another appealing reason for employing ARIMA techniques. With ARIMA techniques, the researcher has the option of modeling several types of intervention models. With econometric modeling, only one type of intervention can be presented, namely, a step function. With ARIMA Intervention analysis, at least three different types of interventions can be modeled. For example, an excise tax increase may have an abrupt effect, with sales gradually returning to their previous pretax increase level. It is also possible that the effect was a gradual but permanent decline. Employing ARIMA Intervention analysis enables the researcher not only to investigate a variety of possible phenomena but to determine what precise effect a public policy measure had on either the sales or the price of cigarettes.

In Chapter 4, I will analyze the effects that the public policy measures of the second wave of regulation (advertising bans and smoking prohibition laws) had on cigarette sales. Since states have a variety of antismoking laws and excise tax rates, there has to be a rationale for choosing which states are to be studied. The method I chose classifies the fifty states using two categories: the number of smoking prohibition laws and level of the state's cigarette excise tax.

These two categories were in turn broken down into three classifica-
tions (low, medium, high); therefore, the resulting matrix has nine
cells (3 by 3 matrix). I chose a variety of states using this matrix so
as to receive the proper mix of different strategies employed by the
states.

Chapter 5 examines the effects of the major public policy measure
of the third wave of regulation, namely, the cigarette excise tax. The
same rationale that was used for choosing states in Chapter 4 will
be used again in Chapter 5. However, I updated this chart so as to
provide the reader with an interesting view of how much the second
and third waves of regulation really do differ. In the first part of
Chapter 5, we will examine the effects that various types of cigarette
excise tax hikes have on cigarette sales. This chapter will also test
the hypotheses that revolve around Jeffrey Harris's contention (1987)
that the cigarette firms use excise tax increases as an excuse to impose
even higher price increases than they normally would.

Chapter 6 will provide a unique look into the world of public
finance. The cigarette excise tax is a major source of revenue for state
governments. But because the cigarette excise tax is also used to
discourage cigarette use, public policy makers face a dilemma in
trying to determine what is the appropriate level of taxation for
cigarettes. Do they have to trade off their need for revenue versus
their concern for health issues? The first part of this chapter will
examine whether or not a Laffer effect exists for cigarette excise tax.
In other words, will cigarette excise tax revenues actually fall if the
cigarette excise tax rate is raised high enough to discourage cigarette
use? The second part of this chapter will analyze the relationship
between various states in setting cigarette excise tax rates. Do states
compete with one another in trying to attract cigarette smokers into
buying cigarettes in their states? Will a neighboring state deliberately
maintain or even lower its cigarette excise tax rate to attract smokers
and hence revenue from a neighboring state with higher cigarette
excise tax rates? Does such strategy actually pay off for a neighboring
"raiding" state?

While the American cigarette industry has undergone rapid change
over the past thirty years, there has been equally rapid change in the
cigarette industry worldwide. Many countries are now faced with the
question of what to do with their previously nationalized cigarette
firms. Chapter 7 will discuss the various options these countries have
and the pros and cons of these options. The chapter will end by
focusing on a fascinating case study of the Spanish cigarette firm,
Tabacalera. Spain's decision to privatize Tabacalera provides an interesting example of the problems facing the cigarette industry worldwide.

Chapter 8 summarizes the results of the ARIMA analysis and reviews the intended and unintended consequences of these government interventions affecting the cigarette industry. The final section of this chapter contains recommendations and predictions concerning the future of the cigarette industry both in the United States and worldwide.

It is hoped that other researchers, policy makers in both the public and private sectors, and observers of business–government relations find the results and observations of this book to be useful and provocative.

2

The History of Government Regulation of the Cigarette Industry: A Three-Wave Model

INTRODUCTION

The American cigarette industry started out as a very small portion of the American tobacco industry. The tobacco industry itself did not become a major economic force until the early 1880s. The industry had to recover from the 1865 increase in the federal excise tax on tobacco products from eleven to thirty-three cents per pound of tobacco, which reduced per capita consumption from 1.3 pounds to 1 pound in the period from 1865 to 1868 (Jacobstein, p. 49). The intent of this excise tax increase was to raise funds to pay for Civil War debt. While it certainly did this, it had the unintended effect of decreasing the consumption of tobacco. Even at this time, government was faced with the question of whether it was trying to raise revenue or control tobacco consumption through its imposition of excise taxes. Although these outcomes are not mutually exclusive, we will see how this dual purpose for excise taxes complicates the modern debate over whether these taxes are "fair" or "just."

By 1890, sales of smoking and chewing tobacco had doubled from their 1865 levels, and cigar sales had trebled. By 1905, it was estimated that the annual expenditure on the 400 million pounds of tobacco products was nearly 500 million dollars. Cigars contributed 70 percent of this sum and smoking, chewing, and snuff about 27 percent. The $1.5 million spent on cigarettes made up only 3 percent of the total expenditures spent on tobacco products (Jacobstein, p. 52). Yet, sixty years later, almost 1.43 billion pounds of tobacco (85 percent of all tobacco consumed) was used in the making of cigarettes. The remaining 15 percent was divided evenly between cigars, snuff, and chewing products. The total combined expenditure in 1964 was well over ten times that of 1905, at about 6 billion dollars after taking inflation into account (Finger, p. 119). Hence, the first sixty years of the cigarette industry were characterized by spectacular growth. Yet the manner in which this growth was achieved became a source of great concern for government, for the oligopolistic structure of the cigarette industry, along with its accompanying collusive pricing strategies, became a target of frequent government action.

Between 1964 and 1984, cigarette sales grew less than 1 percent per year, although margins on sales increased to about twenty cents on every sales dollar (Finger, p. 165). The cigarette industry seems to have developed into the classic cash cow—slow growth but immensely profitable. The slowdown in growth can be attributed to the Surgeon General's report of 1964, which linked cigarette smoking with lung cancer. This report also changed the relationship between government and the cigarette industry. It became a goal of at least some levels and branches of government to reduce cigarette consumption. It is in this era that warning labels were put on cigarette packages and a total ban on cigarette advertising on TV and radio was instituted. No longer was the primary goal of the federal government to police the pricing policies of the cigarette firms but in many cases to reduce sales.

From 1982 to 1993, cigarette sales declined at the rate of 1 percent per year, but profits continue to increase at about 1 percent per year. Moreover, in 1994, cigarette sales actually increased (*The Economist*, March 11, 1995, p. 61). But whether sales were decreasing or increasing, the cigarette industry has experienced increasing profits no matter what direction sales have taken.

In 1985, however, the smoking and health issue was reinforced with the advent of the "passive smoking" issue. No longer could the effects of smoking cigarettes be confined to just the individual smoker. Studies showed that people living in a household with smokers also had a higher incidence of cancer than nonsmokers who lived in a smokeless home. With the emergence of the "passive smoking" issue, the activities of the antismoking groups such as GASP, ASH, and STAT become considerably more intense and a new era of public policy toward smoking began. No longer were critics concerned with regulating the pricing practices of the cigarette firms or trying to reduce cigarette sales gradually. Since 1985, they have been calling on government at both the federal and state levels to virtually abolish the cigarette industry.

Hence, the cigarette industry has experienced three waves of government regulatory activity throughout the hundred years of its existence. A summary comparison of these waves, and the groups involved in each of them, is displayed in Table 2.1. The rest of this chapter will

Table 2.1   The three waves of regulation of the cigarette industry.

	1st Wave: 1911 to 1963	2nd Wave: 1964 to 1985	3rd Wave:1985 to present
Economic	Structure of Industry Pricing Policies of Cigarette firms	Effectiveness of Public Policy Diversification Strategy	Effectiveness of Public Policy Structure of Industry
Political	Implementation of Antitrust Laws Price Supports	Power of SE Congressional Delegation Federal Regulations	Decline of Tobacco Lobby State and Local Regulations
Social	---------------	Effects of Smoking on the Smoker Antismoking Bills	Effects of Smoking on the nonsmoker Eliminate Smoking

examine the various business strategies that the cigarette firms developed to deal with each of the three waves of regulation.

THE FIRST WAVE (1911–1964):
THE STRUCTURE OF THE INDUSTRY

Pre-1911—The Duke Trust

Competition enjoyed a short and very turbulent existence in the American tobacco industry. The person who brought order to the chaotic competition of the 1880s was James B. Duke. Duke's objective was to garner all of the various tobacco products under one trust, or combine, known as the American Tobacco Company. He succeeded in his objective so well that his trust became one of the first targets of the Sherman Anti-Trust Act. In 1911, the Justice Department won a landmark decision breaking up the trust. Yet even after the breakup of the trust, in no sense could one say that competition existed in the cigarette industry. There are a number of reasons for the failure to establish competition, but the chief reason lies with the nature of the trust and the industry that Duke created. The methods which Duke used to establish his tobacco empire are in some ways still being employed by the cigarette firms today. Therefore, it does behoove us once again to review the rise of the Duke tobacco combine.

James Duke, along with his brothers, had been in the smoking tobacco field for seven years when it was apparent that their brand of smoking tobacco, Bull Durham, would not be the number one smoking tobacco in the United States. Duke did not want to play second to anyone, and so he looked to the small but highly disorganized cigarette field where he could become number one in the industry. In the early 1880s, the annual expenditures on cigarettes was estimated to be at most $1.5 million per year, or less than 3 percent of total tobacco sales (Jacobstein, 1907, p. 46). This was one reason why there were so few producers in the emerging cigarette industry. Another reason for this lack of competitors in the evolving cigarette industry was that it required a fairly substantial investment in patented machinery. However, the advantage that cigarette makers had over other branches of the tobacco business was that their labor costs were one-tenth of those for other tobacco products. Hence, the early cigarette industry consisted of four firms that controlled 90 percent of the small but profitable cigarette market.

In 1884, Duke entered the cigarette market, with a rather modest sum of $100,000, which hardly impressed the existing cigarette firms. But in 1887, after borrowing $800,000, Duke deliberately initiated a costly advertising campaign and employed cutthroat pricing tactics that brought him to the forefront of the cigarette industry. By 1889, independence seemed to be a very costly luxury for his rivals, so that by 1890 all of the firms had "merged," and Duke had control of over 90 percent of the market (Jacobstein, p. 107). New Jersey was chosen for incorporation, and Duke's American Tobacco Company was born. Duke's new tobacco trust was enormously successful. In 1890, the profit margin on cigarette sales was about 10 percent, and this was to increase to about 25 percent by 1911. American Tobacco controlled over 90 percent of the cigarette market throughout this period (1890–1911) and at the time of the breakup of the trust had 96 percent of the market. By 1895, American Tobacco paid its preferred dividends, built a surplus of $8 million, and paid a common stock dividend of between 8 percent and 12 percent (ibid., p. 109). Indeed, Duke was number one in cigarettes and was now ready for the challenge of becoming number one in the whole tobacco industry.

With the help of its cigarette profits and through the use of the same tactics that built the cigarette monopoly (economies of scale, heavy advertising, and cutthroat pricing), the American Tobacco Company rapidly gained control of all other tobacco fields except cigars. Mr. Duke even went international by invading the British market using the same tactics he had used in the United States. Imperial Tobacco of Great Britain sued for peace and agreed to form the British-American Tobacco Co. whose task was to market cigarettes throughout the British empire. As part of the agreement, American Tobacco received two-thirds of the profits of the new firm and both home markets were left to their respective domestic companies. But while Duke viewed his consolidation of the tobacco industry as a personal triumph, officials in the U.S. Justice Department viewed with alarm the monopoly he had formed and so decided to take action to rectify the situation.

The Cigarette Industry (1911–1964)

In May 1911, the Supreme Court ruled that Duke's Tobacco Trust was a monopoly in violation of the Sherman Anti-Trust Act and ordered that it be dissolved into a number of separate companies. This decree divided the business of the trust into fourteen independent companies. Table 2.2 summarizes the status of the largest concerns after the trust was dissolved.

Although the trust was broken up into fourteen different entities, it is fairly obvious that the net result of the government's antitrust activity was the creation of an oligopoly that in many respects still forms the basic structure of the cigarette industry today. Duke's American Tobacco was given the most generous "settlement" and R. J. Reynolds became very much the struggling young cousin. However, all of this was to change dramatically within two years of the dissolution of the trust. The reason for this change involved the rise of the cigarette. In 1911, cigarettes still only accounted for less than 6 percent of all tobacco sales. With the breakup of the Duke Trust, three firms accounted for over 80 percent of the cigarette market, with Reynolds not producing

Table 2.2   Percentage of market share after the breakup
of the "tobacco trust." *Source:* Nichols, p. 31

Company	Cigarettes	Smoking Tobacco	Fine Cut	Cigars
The Trust (1910)	86.1	76.2	79.7	14.4
American	37.1	33.1	9.9	6.1
Ligget & Myers	27.8	20.1	- - - -	- - - -
Lorillard	15.3	22.8	27.8	5.7
Reynolds	- - - -	2.7	41.6	- - - -
Big Four	80.2	78.7	79.3	11.8

any cigarettes. But in 1913, using its chewing tobacco profits, Reynolds introduced Camel as a "Turkish and Domestic Blend." The success of Camel was phenomenal. By 1917, cigarette sales had increased by over 500 percent with Camel claiming 34.7 percent of this market. With Camel, Reynolds had found a formula for greatly expanding not only its own but the entire cigarette market: national distribution based upon large-scale national advertising on a *single* brand. Reynolds's strategy was to establish a nationwide reputation through advertising and cut prices while introducing the brand. While American Tobacco might have originated with James Duke, it was Reynolds that used his formula for success after 1911.

The other firms in the industry eventually followed Reynolds's lead. American Tobacco introduced Lucky Strike in 1917, and Liggett & Myers developed Chesterfield in 1918. All of these brands used the Camel formula, that is, concentrating advertising on just the one brand and avoiding price competition. Reynolds was acknowledged as the price leader, and the other firms set their prices accordingly. By 1925 these three brands alone accounted for 82 percent of the national cigarette consumption. Lorillard was the backward cousin that did not develop a domestic blend cigarette (Old Gold) until 1926, by which time its market share had fallen to less than 2 percent. Table 2.3 provides a summary of the market shares of the various firms during the First Wave.

Table 2.3 Percentage of cigarette market share (1913 to 1965). *Source:* Tennant (1913 to 1949), *Business Week* (1955 to 1965)

Year	Reynolds	PM	B&W	American	Lorillard	L&M
1913	.2	---	---	35.3	22.1	34.1
1925	41.6	.5	---	21.3	1.9	26.6
1930	28.6	.4	.2	37.6	6.9	25.0
1939	23.7	7.1	10.6	23.5	5.8	21.6
1949	26.3	9.2	5.9	31.3	5.0	20.2
1955	25.8	8.5	10.5	32.9	6.1	15.6
1960	32.1	9.4	10.4	26.1	10.6	11.3
1965	32.6	10.5	13.3	25.7	9.2	8.7

The other obvious change that took place during this period was the appearance of two other cigarette manufacturers, Philip Morris and Brown & Williamson. By 1964, the sales of both these two firms accounted for nearly 24 percent of the market. These sales came at the expense of the two backward cousins, Lorillard and Liggett & Myers. Still, the overall structure of the industry had not changed since 1913, with Reynolds and American being the dominant players and price setters.

In 1941, the federal government initiated antitrust action against the cigarette industry. The Justice Department won the suit when the Supreme Court in 1946 ruled that the industry had violated Section 2 of the Sherman Act by attempting to monopolize the cigarette market by their tobacco leaf (where they had a monopsonistic position) and their pricing policies. Once again, however, the ruling had little effect on the structure of the cigarette industry since none of the firms were required to divest themselves of any holdings or market share (Nichols, p. 247).

Is the cigarette industry a natural oligopoly? Can the government actually foster competition in this industry? Two economists who attempted to answer these questions were Richard Tennant (1950) and William Nichols (1951), and they came up with quite different conclusions and suggestions.

Tennant's *The American Cigarette Industry* was an outgrowth of his doctoral dissertation at Yale. Tennant was the first of many economists to estimate the elasticity of demand for cigarettes; he found the demand to be quite inelastic, and this finding has remained valid even today. He maintained that the oligopolistic structure of the cigarette industry was "natural" because of the economies of scale needed both to manufacture cigarettes and because of the high cost of conducting the national advertising used to sell cigarettes. His overall conclusion (1950) was:

> Although there is an usually good opportunity to reform the structure of the industry and although there is ample precedent in this industry for legal measures to secure greater decentralization, we do not find that it would be economically desirable or, accordingly to political criteria, very urgent. (p. 385)

Meanwhile, Nichols's *Price Policies in the Cigarette Industry* is much more of a reformist or populist view of the cigarette industry. Nichols concentrates his efforts on the plight of the tobacco farmer. He was the first to use the term "monopsony" (many sellers and only a few buyers) to describe the relationship between the cigarette industry and the thousands of tobacco growers. Nichols agrees wholeheartedly with the Supreme Court decision of 1946 that a conspiracy did exist but that the economic damage that had occurred was suffered primarily by the tobacco farmers and the consumers of cigarettes. His policy recommendations included the dissolution of the cigarette industry with the federal government taking over the manufacturing and distribution of cigarettes, social control of advertising, and the revision of cigarette excise taxes (Nichols, 1951, p. 321).

Obviously, the conclusions that Tennant and Nichols arrived at were quite different. Yet the arguments that were used during this period (1911–1964) are still being echoed today. From one side, the argument is made that the cigarette industry is efficient, highly profitable, and contributes billions of dollars to the U.S. economy. Meanwhile, opponents of the industry maintain that the cigarette industry not only produces a deadly product that society could do without but also makes unconscionable profits by taking advantage not only of their customers but also their suppliers—the tobacco farmers.

Although the issues that were the cause for governmental action during the First Wave are still operative even today, the issue that separates the First Wave from the other two waves of government regulation of the cigarette industry is the emergence of the smoking and health issue. It is now time to examine how the government and the cigarette industry responded to the demands for more regulation of this industry due to the emergence of the smoking and health issue.

THE SECOND WAVE (1964–1985):
THE HEALTH OF THE SMOKER

If the driving force behind the First Wave for both government action and the pricing policies of the cigarette firms was the structure of the cigarette industry, the impetus for the Second Wave was undoubtedly the smoking and health issue. In 1964, the Surgeon General published a report which concluded that "cigarette smoking is a health hazard of sufficient importance in the United States to warrant remedial action" (*Surgeon General*, 1964, p. 231). The nature of these "remedial" actions and how the cigarette industry reacted to them will be the focus of this section.

As the antismoking sentiment increased throughout the country, it was the Congress (as opposed to the executive branch, which initiated action during the First Wave) that responded to the demand for more regulation of the cigarette industry. No longer was the chief concern of government the structure of the cigarette industry but with ways of reducing the number of smokers and hence, cigarette sales. The executive branch of the federal government was divided throughout this period with the Surgeon General's office, HEW, and the FTC wishing to take further actions against the industry and the Departments of Agriculture and Commerce leading the opposition to any further restrictive measures. The executive branch was throughout this period (1964–1985) extremely sensitive about further alienating tobacco interests and never gave its full support to any of the antismoking measures proposed.

The chief measures enacted by Congress during this era were the Cigarette Warning Label Act of 1966, the TV and Radio Cigarette Advertising Ban of 1971, and finally the doubling of the federal excise tax on cigarettes in 1983. The rest of this section will examine the rationale behind these public policy actions and the strategies that cigarette makers developed to deal with these new public policy initiatives.

PUBLIC POLICY MEASURES DURING THE SECOND WAVE

Cigarette Warning Label Requirement

"Cigarette smoking may be hazardous to your health "
(Public Law 89–92, 15, USC)

For antismoking forces, the requirement that cigarette makers include a warning on the packages of their product was the opening salvo in their campaign against cigarette smoking. The rationale behind this warning label was simply to remind cigarette smokers continuously that cigarette smoking was dangerous and therefore the cigarette smoker ought to consider giving up the habit. The effect this measure had on cigarette sales will be examined in Chapter 4.

Even though the warning requirement was considered to be extremely mild, another benefit, at least from the standpoint of the antismoking groups, was that the government had finally committed itself to an official position on the dangers of smoking. The issue had been brought to the congressional agenda and a victory had been won. For the first time, the tobacco lobby had been defeated. The long-term effect of this victory was to legitimize the smoking and health issue as an object for vigorous public policy experimentation and public debate.

Yet the passage of this measure has often been portrayed as a Pyrrhic victory for the antismoking forces. Although the warning label requirement was opposed vigorously by the industry, it did have one curious benefit for the industry. Over the years, many suits have been filed against cigarette firms claiming that the product is a dangerous one and therefore these firms should be liable as a result of selling this dangerous product. In the past, the courts have ruled that smokers did know of the dangers of cigarette smoking, particularly because of the warning label requirement. However, in the famous Cipollone case, a New Jersey judge ruled against the cigarette firms. But even though the court held the cigarette firms liable, it still rewarded the plaintiff only $400,000 (*Wall Street Journal*, 6/4/88, p. 1). So it remains to be seen how successful this "warning label" defense will be in the future for the cigarette firms and how the antismoking forces propose to attack it (*New York Times*, 6/14/88, p. D1).

The Ban on TV and Radio Advertising

On January 1, 1971, cigarette advertising on TV and radio was banned as a result of the Public Health Cigarette Smoking Act of 1969. The ban was hailed as a major victory by the antismoking forces. The rationale behind this legislation was that cigarette advertising stimulated sales and therefore, if advertising was banned, cigarette sales would fall. The effect that this advertising ban had on cigarette sales will be examined in further detail in Chapter 4.

There have been previous studies trying to measure the effect of this ban on cigarette sales. Both Bass (1969) and Hamilton (1972), using somewhat similar econometric models and national data, disputed the claim of the antismoking forces. Hamilton maintained that cigarette consumption actually increased because of this action since the broadcasters could no longer be required to broadcast antismoking spots. The influence of the smoking and health controversy was dampened and the cigarette firms had ironically once again won. Hamilton's conclusion offers a sober assessment about the effectiveness of the advertising ban:

> Actions that intensified the health scare would have been a more effective policy than banning advertising. . . . Policymakers must evaluate policy models carefully. Action based on wishful thinking seldom is as effective as that based on carefully specified models accurately depicting the forces influencing the policy objectives and connections between forces and proposed policy actions. (p. 409)

Doubling the Federal Cigarette Excise Tax (1983)

The excise tax is the most frequently employed weapon in the antismoking movement's arsenal. There is a twofold rationale behind this policy measure: first, since the excise tax raises the price of cigarettes, it is thought to prevent people, particularly teenagers, from starting to smoke; second, the cigarette excise generates tremendous revenues for the federal, state, and local governments. For example, in 1993, almost $26 billion was collected by government at all levels through cigarette excise taxes (Tobacco Institute, *The Tax Burden on*

Tobacco, p. iii). Hence, the cigarette excise tax is considered a "sin" tax, one where the government "does well, while doing good."

Although this tax does indeed raise substantial revenue for government, there are two other major factors that are debated in regard to this tax. First, there is the "fairness" issue. Opponents of the tax, particularly the Tobacco Institute, claim that the tax is regressive and a way in which government legislates morality (Tobacco Institute, *The Excise Tax: The Fairness Issue*, pp. 2, 3). Meanwhile, supporters of the tax maintain that government ought to penalize those who smoke since their health costs are significantly higher than those of nonsmokers and it is the government that ultimately assumes these social costs. The ethical argument surrounding the excise tax is the same one that shrouds the smoking and health issue in general, namely, the right of a person to smoke versus the cost of this activity not only to the smoker but to society in general. Chapter 3 will examine how this ethical debate is reflected in the public policy decision process.

The second argument surrounding the excise tax issue is the effectiveness of this tax in reducing cigarette sales. This has been studied extensively by economists. It is generally agreed that the demand for cigarettes is inelastic and that Tennant's estimate for elasticity of between $-.4$ and $-.5$ is still accurate today. Therefore, one might expect that the same would be true of the excise tax, that is, only a large increase in the cigarette excise tax will produce a decrease in cigarette sales. Economists who have studied this issue have based their studies on European data, which show a uniform excise tax rate that is not the case in the United States. For example, Chappel (1984) and Leu (1984) used econometric models to estimate the effect that excise taxes had on cigarette consumption in various countries (France, Belgium, and Great Britain). The general conclusion of these studies was that these increases in the excise tax rate were not great enough to have a significant impact on cigarette consumption. As for the effect of the doubling of the federal excise tax rate in 1983, there has been little work done on this other than an estimate by the Congressional Budget Office (CBO) based on national data indicating that the tax increase had no permanent effect on consumption (*CBO*, 1985, p. 74). Hence, the question that needs to be investigated is, How much would the cigarette excise tax have to be raised in order to affect cigarette sales adversely? This issue will also be analyzed in Chapter 5.

So far we have reviewed the various public policy measures that were enacted during the Second Wave of regulation. The rest of this chapter will deal with the business and corporate strategies that cigarette firms used to cope with their hostile external environment.

THE STRATEGY AND STRUCTURE OF THE CIGARETTE INDUSTRY DURING THE SECOND WAVE OF REGULATION

The smoking and health issue has had and continues to have a tremendous impact on both the strategies of the cigarette firms and the structure of the cigarette industry. Unlike the First Wave of government intervention, these issues did indeed change not only the strategies of the cigarette firms but also the structure of the cigarette industry. Before 1964, cigarette sales had grown at least 3 percent per year. After 1964, this sales growth rate slowed. For the first time in its history, the cigarette industry faced declining sales for more than one year, when sales declined by an average of 1 percent from 1982 until 1993. While this decline in cigarette sales was radical enough, it was the way in which the smoking and health issue changed the business and corporate strategies of the individual cigarette firms and subsequently the structure of the cigarette industry. These strategic and structural changes will be the focus of the rest of this chapter.

As mentioned earlier, during the First Wave (1911–1964), nonfiltered cigarettes were very popular and there was little need for product innovation. Because consumers tended to stick to one brand throughout their smoking "careers," advertising and marketing strategies were aimed at attracting and keeping new smokers. This changed with the advent of the smoking and health issue, and only those firms that could adapt to the new environment would prosper.

Responding to the health concerns of their customers, the cigarette firms introduced various brands to satisfy the consumers' desire for a "healthy" cigarette. This change in consumers' desires forced cigarette firms to "diversify" their product offerings to satisfy the variety of consumer tastes. Filtered cigarettes, such as Marlboro, Winston, and Viceroy, which were presumed to be less hazardous to the smoker's health, surged in popularity; filtered menthol brands also began to flourish. After the rise of the filter cigarette, the "low tar" brands of cigarettes were introduced. Then, in the early 1970s, new brands were targeted at such market segments as women (Virginia Slims) and the black population (Merit). The result of this effort to target the needs of smokers was an extremely segmented market with a dramatic increase in the number of brands. No longer the simple promoters of several well-known brands, the cigarette firms had to become masters of marketing and advertising. As can be seen from Figure 2.1, the two firms that became the experts at marketing and producing not only the less hazardous cigarette but a cigarette for every taste were R. J. Reynolds and Philip Morris.

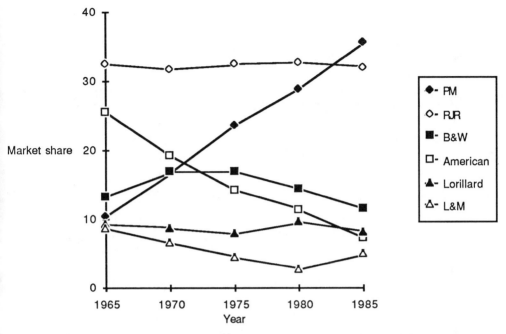

Figure 2.1 Cigarette market share (1965 to 1985). *Source: Business Week* (1965 to 1985)

The period from 1964 to 1985 was thus one of great change in the cigarette industry. The marketing strategies of the firms changed from promoting one basic brand to showering the public with various brands to satisfy a variety of tobacco needs and tastes. The structure of the industry also changed radically. The firms that learned to diversify their product lines most effectively were awarded market share. By far, the two firms that adapted themselves to this new environment were Philip Morris and RJR. Because of their success, Philip Morris and RJR had formed a duopoly that had cornered almost 73 percent of the cigarette market (*Business Week*, 1/18/85, p. 90).

What is even more striking is how all of these firms also used "diversification" as the basis of their corporate strategy during this Second Wave of regulation. This corporate strategy allowed these firms to use their considerable assets (1) to continue the battle over the domestic cigarette market share and therefore "milk" this lucrative market; and (2) to acquire new companies and new products, that is, to become less dependent upon cigarettes. How successful have these firms been in fulfilling these goals? Each of the "Big Six" cigarette firms will now be examined.

Philip Morris (PM)

No company in the cigarette industry succeeded as well in the 1970s and 1980s as Philip Morris. During this Second Wave of regulation, PM grew from the fourth largest cigarette firm in the United States to become the fifth largest firm in the Fortune 500. The company was successful in pursuing the goals of obtaining additional market share in the domestic cigarette market (it has more than doubled in size since 1970) and it acquired assets that increased its size more than ten times. Yet there are problems as well, particularly with the goal of "diversification."

Cigarettes. Philip Morris became the largest domestic producer of cigarettes, overtaking its chief rival, RJR in 1983. In 1985, PM had sales of 215.2 billion cigarettes, 37.9 percent of the domestic cigarette market and a 2 percent increase in market share since 1983 (*Business Week*, 1/18/85, p. 89). PM's continuous rise in the domestic cigarette market can be directly attributed to the success of the Marlboro brand, which accounted for nearly 21 percent of the entire domestic cigarette market in 1985. PM's other successful brands are Benson & Hedges (4.38 percent), Merit (4.36 percent), and Virginia Slims (2.89 percent) (ibid., 1/18/85, p. 90). It is somewhat ironic that while success in this market is thought to be achieved by offering a great number of brands, in actuality the old strategy of focusing on one brand of cigarettes has worked well even in the age of the smoking and health issue.

Another trend that was started during this period was the "internationalization" of cigarette firms. This trend toward finding new foreign markets will be studied under the Third Wave of regulation. It was at the end of this Second Wave of regulation that PM made its first big venture into foreign markets with the opening of a cigarette production plant in China in 1985.

Beer. Like its other cigarette rivals, Philip Morris's other major corporate goal is "diversification." PM was once again a leader for the cigarette industry in this area, as PM began to diversify as early as 1957 when it acquired Miliprint Industries, a small packaging firm. However, its diversification program began in earnest when PM acquired Miller Beer in 1971. With Miller, PM could use the same strategy that it had employed in the cigarette market. If the 1970s were the era of the "healthy" cigarette, then the 1970s also provided the opportunity for the "healthy" beer, namely, Miller Lite. PM's advertising for Miller Lite in some ways paralleled the one which it employed for Marlboro. The Marlboro man assured the "macho" male that a filtered cigarette was indeed a "real" cigarette. With Miller Lite, the use of ex-athletes assured the beer drinker that Lite was really a "man's beer." This campaign proved to be so successful that Miller Lite is now the second largest-selling beer in the United States. Miller continued to use the cigarette strategy of PM when it segmented its market: Lowenbrau, the second largest selling super-premium, was acquired in 1979; in 1983 and 1984, respectively, Meister Brau and Milwaukee's Best were introduced in the "popular" price segment of the U.S. beer market (*Philip Morris Annual Report 1986*, p. 5).

Philip Morris was hoping to transfer the same tactic it had used in the cigarette industry to the beer industry, namely, segmenting the market. Yet this technique, although at first successful, has not proven to be quite the formula for success that it was for cigarettes.

One reason for this halt in the growth of Miller's sales can be attributed to the continuing decline of Miller High Life, Miller's original flagship, which has lost 60% of its sales volume since 1981 (*Business Week*, 2/1/88, p. 26). In the cigarette industry, PM found it possible to segment the market without affecting its brand leader, Marlboro. Apparently, market segmentation is not as easily accomplished in the beer industry. The industry leader, Anheuser-Busch, has managed to not only survive the rise of Miller but has managed to increase its market share to 39.7 percent, mainly on the strength of its one brand, Budweiser (ibid., p. 26).

Foods. Philip Morris has made other acquisitions, most notably its purchase of Seven-Up in 1980. With Seven-Up, PM once again tried to use its "healthy" product strategy (the Un-Cola theme) but without much success and therefore sold Seven-Up in 1986.

In 1985, PM undertook its most daring diversification project when it purchased General Foods. With the acquisition of General Foods, Philip Morris became the largest consumer-products company in the United States, with $23 billion in annual sales. With this purchase, assets increased from $3.6 billion to $5.9 billion, and sales doubled from $10.1 billion to $20.6 billion. Many have claimed that the $5.7 billion price (3.75 times the book price) was too high. But Hamish Maxwell, the chairman of PM, was attracted to General Foods' success with decaffeinated coffee and other products that catered to "trends" or specialized segments of the food market. Maxwell also explained that PM ought to invest in areas where "experience would lead to sensible [market] judgments," that is, where PM could use its marketing expertise (*Wall Street Journal*, 9/30/85, p. 2). We will examine how PM built on this acquisition of General Foods to become one of the largest food concerns in the world during the Third Wave of regulation.

Table 2.4 PM's various business segments at the end of the Second Wave. *Source:* Philip Morris Inc. Annual Report (1987), p. 1.

Operating Revenue (%)	1987	1986*	1985
Tobacco	53	50	66
Food	36	38	10
Beer	11	12	18
Soft Drink	- - -	- - -	4

Operating Profits (%)	1987	1986*	1985
Tobacco	80	77	90
Food	15	20	4
Beer	4	4	5
Soft Drink	- - -	- - -	0
Other	1	1	1

* = Purchase of General Foods and the sale of Seven-Up

PM's other diversification projects during the Second Wave were rather insignificant when compared to the tobacco, food, and brewing operations. These other ventures include Mission Vijeo Inc., a real estate company engaged in community development mostly centered in Southern California, and Philip Morris Credit Corporation, which provides financing to the various divisions of the corporation. In total, these operations account for less than 1 percent of total revenues and profits of Philip Morris, Inc.

How successful was the diversification strategy of PM from 1964 to 1985? A close examination of Table 2.4 reveals a very mixed picture.

With the acquisition of General Foods, Philip Morris's revenues increased by 63.5 percent. However, profits increased by only 41 percent and would have increased by 18 percent even if General Foods had not been purchased. Total assets increased from $9.339 billion in 1984 to $17.429 billion in 1985—an 87 percent increase in assets. Once again, however, PM's return on assets actually decreased from 25 percent in 1984 to 18 percent in 1985. So, in essence, PM became a much larger, diversified firm but not necessarily a more profitable one. Indeed, the only segment that has shown a continuous increase in profitability over the past five years is tobacco. One could easily accuse the management of Philip Morris of employing what could be termed a "puffer belly" strategy during this period, by making the firm so large and debt ridden that no raider could attempt a leveraged buyout by using the cash flow from the lucrative cigarette segment to pay for the purchase. In fact, one might ask why Philip Morris's management did not start paying additional dividends to stockholders rather than making purchases that appear to be for the most part quite unprofitable.

Thus, for all its acquisitions and mergers, Philip Morris was still essentially a domestic cigarette firm at the end of the Second Wave of regulation, but one that had grown huge. The vast majority of PM's profits came from its domestic cigarette division. No doubt, PM continued to search for the "star" business on which it could lavish its ample cash flow but, in the meanwhile, PM's management was well aware that PM's fortunes rested with the Marlboro man.

RJR Nabisco (RJR)

If Philip Morris's story throughout the 1970s and 1980s was one of exponential growth, the RJR saga was one of continuous success. Throughout its history, RJR has been either the number one or number two cigarette producer in the United States. Like its chief competitor, Philip Morris, RJR implemented a corporate strategy of diversification into the food industry. It was the preceding realization that prompted RJR's CEO, F. Ross Johnson, to rename his firm RJR Nabisco and to move corporate headquarters from Winston-Salem, NC, to Atlanta, GA (*Wall Street Journal*, 1/12/87, p. 1). Johnson stated that his motive for these actions coincides with his belief that RJR should no longer be perceived as a "tobacco company with other interests" (*Fortune*, 7/18/88, p. 37). This analysis will examine how successful RJR was in its effort to become a food industry giant with tobacco interests.

Cigarettes. During the Second Wave, four of RJR's brands—Winston, Salem, Camel, and Vantage—were among the ten largest selling cigarette brands in the United States. Century, introduced by RJR in 1983, was their first entry in the domestic cigarette market featuring twenty-five-cigarette packs, as contrasted to the traditional twenty-cigarette pack. In March 1985, RJR introduced the Ritz cigarette brand, which was developed in association with fashion designer Yves St. Laurent. All of these innovations once again support the contention that RJR is one of the most innovative marketers in the cigarette industry.

Yet, for all of RJR's innovativeness, its market share remained relatively constant throughout the period of 1964 to 1985 and now trails market leader PM by five percentage points (see Figure 2.1). RJR followed Philip Morris's lead entering the international cigarette market. As was the case with Philip Morris, this effort became much more pronounced during the Third Wave of regulation. RJR's efforts in this area will be examined when we turn to analyzing the performance of cigarette firms during the Third Wave.

Food. Diversification is a word that has hardly been foreign to the RJR vocabulary over the years. As early as 1956, RJR's management had amended its corporate charter to permit investment in nontobacco enterprises. The reasons underlying the change in 1956 still pertain today:

> First, having captured one-third of the U.S. cigarette market, the company could see a point of diminishing returns for growth potential. Second, significant cash was being generated which could be invested advantageously elsewhere. (Tilley, p. 231)

With these policy goals in mind, RJR set out to diversify. RJR's diversification policy has differed from PM's diversification policy in two ways: first, RJR was not afraid of purchasing businesses that required expertise outside of its own distinctive competence, marketing; second, RJR's purchases, at least in the early days of diversification, were of small, one-product companies that RJR would merge together, especially those involving foods. RJR's first acquisition (in 1958) involved an aluminum packaging company that was sold in 1982. In 1963, RJR first entered the food industry and over the years has acquired the following products: Vermont Maid Syrups, My-T-Fine Desserts, Chun-King, Patio Foods, and Del Monte (Tilley, p. 214).

In 1969, RJR made its biggest adventure into a nonmarketing industry when it purchased Sea-Land Services, Inc., which was the largest containerized freight shipping operation in the world. Then, in 1970, RJR sought an oil source for its Sea-Land's fleet of ships, and so RJR bought Aminoil, an oil producer, which was part of the Iranian consortium. However, with the Iranian revolution of 1979, RJR's grand oil and shipping plan proved to be a financial nightmare (Tilley, p. 424). After having pumped at least $600 million into these businesses since 1979, RJR sold its fleet of ships to the U.S. Navy in 1984. With the sale of this nonmarketing enterprise, RJR developed an entirely new diversification strategy (*RJR Annual Report 1984*, p. 2).

In 1984, RJR's management announced a new diversification policy: future acquisitions would only be made in the foods and services industries, and these purchases would be substantial (*RJR Annual Re-*

port 1985, p. 2). In 1984, RJR purchased Heublein, Inc., which is engaged
in the production and distribution of alcoholic beverages, including
beer, wine, and "white" spirits (vodka and gin). Later, in 1984, RJR was
still on the prowl for further diversification, and so it purchased Kentucky Fried Chicken (KFC). RJR saw great opportunity in the whole area
of the fast-food industry; KFC had a unique product in this industry
which RJR sought to expand, especially internationally. However, RJR
lost interest both in Heublein and KFC in 1986 and sold both of these
businesses off to finance the acquisition of a food giant, Nabisco, for 3.2
times book value or $4.9 billion (ibid., p. 1).

On January 1, 1986, the operations of Nabisco and all the other food
industries that RJR operated were combined to form one of the world's
largest food operations, Nabisco Brands, Inc. With the addition of
Nabisco, RJR increased its food sales from $3.4 billion to $8.5 billion. In
Nabisco, RJR's management thought that it had finally found a business
into which it could pour its substantial cigarette cash flow. The corporate commitment was reflected in the new corporation's name, RJR
Nabisco. As with PM's purchase of General Foods, the results of this
purchase were at best suspect.

Table 2.5 ought to provide the reader with a clear portrait of the
fundamental structure of RJR. What sort of picture of RJR Nabisco do

Table 2.5   RJR's various business segments at the end of the Second
Wave. *Source:* RJR Nabisco Annual Report (1987), p. 3.

Operating Revenue (%)	1987	1986*	1985
Tobacco	36	37	44
Food	64	63	56

Operating Profits (%)	1987	1986*	1985
Tobacco	65	63	69
Food	35	37	31

* = Purchase of Nabisco Brands

these numbers portray? Clearly, in terms of sales or revenues, RJR Nabisco is no longer a cigarette company. With the purchase of Nabisco in 1986, cigarette sales account for only 37 percent of total sales. However, profits from cigarette sales still constitute more than 63 percent of RJR's profits.

Whereas RJR certainly broadened its product base with the purchase of Nabisco, in no way did it lose its dependency on tobacco for supporting its other business ventures. Although it could be claimed that RJR's diversification program seemed to be a bit more successful than PM's program during this Second Wave of regulation, no one would dispute that PM won the battle for the lucrative cigarette stakes. But it is also obvious that neither of these firms was in any position "to kick the habit" at the end of the Second Wave of regulation. Cigarettes supplied the cash needed to keep their various food and service businesses going in the future. Both used the corporate strategy of diversification to bloat their assets so as to protect themselves from leveraged buyouts. But while PM's management stayed the course in using this "puffer belly" corporate strategy, we will see how RJR's Ross Johnson tried to spin off the tobacco segment to obtain its huge cash flow.

THE LITTLE FOUR: B&W, AMERICAN, LORILLARD, AND L&M

Brown and Williamson (B&W)

Brown and Williamson, the third largest cigarette manufacturer in the United States, was the quietest member of the industry, with almost 10.8 percent of the cigarette market throughout the Second Wave of regulation (*Business Week*, 1/18/88, p. 89). Its chief brand is Kool, which has 6.4 percent of the cigarette market. However, B&W's market share has been steadily declining since 1970, when B&W had nearly 17 percent of the market.

As a subsidiary of the British American Tobacco Co. (BAT), B&W is not required to publish an annual report. Therefore, it is impossible to surmise what percentage of revenues and profits can be attributed to the sale of cigarettes. However, B&W's parent, BAT, started to diversify in the 1970s into specialty paper, retail trade stores, and financial services. In 1986, tobacco accounted for a little under 50 percent of BAT's worldwide earnings, which were estimated to be $2 billion per year. Following the lead of BAT, B&W, using its cash flow, has acquired such retail giants as Gimbels, Saks Fifth Avenue, and numerous small insurance firms.

B&W plodded along in the domestic cigarette market seemingly mired in a distant, third-place position. It continued to use the proceeds of its cigarette sales to invest in businesses in which its parent firm, BAT, had an interest. Although B&W remained a force in the U.S. cigarette industry, it needed to face the question of whether it wanted to make a long-term commitment to the U.S. cigarette market.

American Brands

If PM and RJR are models of success in the cigarette industry, American Brands (Tobacco) has to be considered the corporate also-ran. American failed to respond to the change in the cigarette market in the 1960s, thereby losing its leadership position to RJR in 1966. It was in that year that American executives realized that the old American Tobacco Co. was dying and needed to map a future plan of action if it was to survive. Three familiar courses were decided upon: (1) update the cigarette business by developing a filter cigarette; (2) find a way to build an international cigarette business; (3) use American's considerable cash flow for "meaningful" diversification. How successful has American been at achieving these goals? Table 2.6 ought to be able to provide some answers.

American Brands' diversification attempt could not be classified as highly successful. While overall cigarette sales barely increased, most of this growth took place in the international cigarette market, which

Table 2.6 American Brands' various business segments at the end of the Second Wave. *Source:* American Brands Inc. Annual Report (1987), p. 1.

Operating Revenue (%)	1987	1986	1985
Tobacco	66	61	60
Other*	34	39	40

Operating Profits (%)	1987	1986	1985
Tobacco	67	60	57
Other*	33	40	43

* includes Financial Services, Hardware and Security, Distilled Beverages, Golf and Leisure Equipment, Food Products, Optical Products, Personal Care Products, Office Products

was not nearly as profitable as the domestic cigarette market. In the domestic cigarette market, American does not seem to be able to stem the downward slide it has experienced since 1965. In the twenty-year period from 1965 to 1985, American's market share has fallen from 25.7 percent to 6 percent of the cigarette market. This decline shows no sign of abating in the near future. American's diversification strategy appears to be similar to the one employed by RJR in its early diversification attempts, namely, acquiring smaller companies and assembling them together to build various divisions that range from financial services to golf and leisure products. In fact, American has averaged two acquisitions per year for the past twenty years (*Time*, 1/18/85, p. 71).

For all of this acquisition activity, cigarettes and tobacco still account for nearly 67 percent of American's operating income. But with declining domestic sales and increased competition on the international front, prospects for American Brands are not encouraging. The one bright spot for American is that it has very little debt, its current ratio holding at 1.5 since 1984. Thus, it appeared that American could continue its policy of acquiring smaller consumer-oriented products that require marketing expertise. It is American's hope that eventually one of these firms will turn out to be the "star" on which it can devote its ample cash flow. But it also appears that the firm on which James Duke founded the American cigarette industry will soon be leaving that domestic cigarette industry whether it wants to or not.

Lorillard

The nation's oldest tobacco firm, Lorillard, differs from the other four firms which have been previously examined in that it is no longer in the position of acquiring other firms since it was acquired by Lawrence Tisch in 1970. Lorillard's troubles can be traced back all the way to the 1920s when it failed to come up with a milder blended cigarette. In the 1960s, Lorillard again failed to introduce a "healthy" filter cigarette until it was rather late in that game. As a result, Lorillard has become a small player in the domestic cigarette market and does not even compete in the overseas cigarette market. Yet, even in this lowly position, Lorillard combined increased revenues from price hikes, reduced advertising costs, and a high income-to-sales ratio (characteristics of all cigarette companies) to produce a steady cash income, and with this cash flow the attention of Lawrence Tisch.

What were Tisch's intentions with Lorillard? It seems that Lorillard was acquired to provide the cash needed to finance Tisch's other takeover targets. In 1974, Tisch acquired CNA, an ailing insurance firm, and used funds from Lorillard and from his Loews Theater chain to bring that firm back to financial health. Then, in early 1986, Tisch managed to assemble the cash and financing needed to takeover CBS (*Lexis*, Corporate Summaries, Lorillard, Inc., 1985).

Throughout all this acquisition activity, Tisch did not abandon Lorillard. He did sink $75 million into sorely needed capital improvements in Lorillard's cigarette manufacturing facilities. He also changed Lorillard's advertising strategy so that Lorillard maintained its 8.2 percent of the U.S. cigarette market. This market share produced $275,000,000 in profits in 1985 (*Lexis*, Corporate Summaries, Lorillard, Inc., 1985). Although the above figure is insignificant when compared to the profits that PM and RJR generate in this industry, it does provide Tisch the steady cash he needs to wheel and deal in the U.S. financial community. But given that Lorillard accounts for less than 15 percent in total revenues and income in Tisch's financial empire, it is doubtful that Tisch would show much loyalty to Lorillard if the government enacts severe antismoking measures in the near future.

Ligget and Myers (L&M)

Like Lorillard, Ligget and Myers is a cigarette firm that has been losing market share since the 1920s. L&M also failed to respond to the market call for a "healthy" cigarette. L&M 's market share has fallen from 15.6 percent in 1960 to less than 4 percent in 1985.

Yet, despite its cigarette woes, L&M has proven to be skilled at the diversification game. L&M started to diversify in 1964 with the purchase of Alpo dog food and along the way has picked up such other household names as Grand Marnier Liqueur and Wild Turkey bourbon. In 1985, nontobacco operations provided 70 percent of operating revenues and 91 percent of operating income (*Lexis*, Corporate Summaries, Liggett Group, 1985).

In 1980, Grand Metropolitan bought L&M and renamed it the Ligget Group. It appears that Grand Metropolitan had only a short-run interest in the Ligget group. Although Grand Met was quite content to use the cash flow from Ligget operations, it had no great desire to become involved in another controversial industry. Hence, Grand Met was more than willing to sell the Ligget Group as soon as a buyer was found.

Summary of the Second Wave

The driving force behind the Second Wave of regulation of the cigarette industry was the smoking and health issue. We have just seen how this issue forced various strategic changes by the firms; they segmented the cigarette market, they began establishing foreign markets, and above all they sought to diversify their assets. These strategic changes by the various cigarette firms led in turn to changes in the structure of this industry. In 1965, American and RJR were the dominant forces in the cigarette market, with almost 58 percent of the market between them, while the rest of the competitors split the remaining part of the market.

However, by the time of the end of this Second Wave of regulation, the structure of the cigarette industry was quite different. The U.S. cigarette market was now almost totally dominated by two giants, PM and RJR Nabisco. In essence, the cigarette industry had become a duopoly with well over 75 percent of the total cigarette market. While pursuing similar corporate strategies, these two firms were still dependent on cigarettes for at least two-thirds of their profits. Hence, neither of these firms, which rank fifth (PM) and twelfth (RJR) in the Fortune 500, could realistically plan to leave this market if they hope to continue their diversification plans (*Fortune*, 4/12/88, p. 169). It was and is a market that these cigarette giants will not and cannot surrender willingly no matter how much government pressure is applied upon them to exit.

Meanwhile, the other four producers of cigarettes (B&W, American, Lorillard, and L&M) certainly do not have the same stakes as the two largest producers in staying in this market. Their loyalty to the cigarette cause is at best tenuous. One indicator of the degree to which a firm is committed to supporting this industry can be found in the amount contributed to the Tobacco Institute. In 1986, PM and RJR provided well over 80 percent of the funds that supported the Tobacco Institute's activities (*Fortune*, 8/17/87, p. 71). Although none of these firms is about to immediately abandon this lucrative business, neither does it appear that they will fight any further government interventions into their industry with any great vigor.

THE THIRD WAVE: THE RIGHTS OF THE NONSMOKER (1986 TO THE PRESENT)

On December 20, 1985, Surgeon General C. Everett Koop announced the results of new research by his staff on the effects of smoking. One of the findings of this report indicated that there was a significant increase in the rate of lung cancer among nonsmokers in households where nonsmokers were living with cigarette smokers (*Surgeon General's Report*, 12/20/85, p. 1). This report sparked off a flurry of medical activity into the phenomenon called "passive smoking" or the "secondary effects" of smoking.

With the Surgeon General's report, the "rights of the nonsmoker" were raised anew by antismoking groups. No longer could it be claimed that smoking harms only the individual smoker and hence it is the smoker's right to smoke or not to smoke. This issue gave antismoking forces an entirely new way of arguing their case against smoking. With the passive smoking issue, nonsmokers can claim that smoking affects their health even if they do not smoke. Although the groups involved in this Third Wave have not changed significantly from the Second Wave, there is a profound difference in both the level of intensity and broad appeal that the passive smoking issue has brought to the smoking and health debate. This will be examined in much greater detail in Chapter 3 but suffice it to say that the "passive" smoking issue invigorated the antismoking movement with new drive and zeal.

Traditionally, the antismoking movement was led by groups such as the American Cancer Society, American Lung Association, and American Medical Association, which in the past tended to be politically cautious and to be much more willing to strike political compromises. The federal agencies that handled the smoking and health issue include HS, the Surgeon General, and the Office of Smoking and Health. Again, because of the political sensitivity of these issues, these bodies advocated, for the most part, noncontroversial solutions to the smoking and health problem, especially during election periods, and were ready to settle for less than an ideal solution.

But with the rise of the passive smoking issue comes the emergence of activist groups such as ASH, GASP, and STAT that are dedicated solely to the antismoking movement. The rhetoric and tone of these groups is much more strident than that of more established multi-issue health organizations. These groups consider themselves as crusaders against an evil empire, namely, the cigarette industry. Inflammatory phrases such the "The Six Murderers" (used by STAT) are used to describe the cigarette firms, and mottoes such as "Sue the Bastards" decorate the office of John Banzhaf, the executive director of ASH (Troyer and Markle, 1986, p. 66). As the rhetoric has grown more hostile, strong antismoking language has even crept into the federal establishment. The Surgeon General has said, "Smoking is the single most important preventable cause of death" (*Surgeon General's Report*, 1986, p. 2), declared that cigarette smoking is an "addiction" (*Surgeon General's Report*, 1988, p. 1), and stated a national goal of a smoke-free society by the Year 2000.

It is interesting to note that the antismoking rhetoric has also become much more "normative" in tone. Smoking is wrong and ought to be wiped out. No longer is the cigarette industry confronted with an antismoking argument based solely on a cost-benefit analysis; it now faces what some have called an "ideology of anti-smoking" (Berger, 1986, p. 234). The goal upon which this ideology is built is the utopian dream of a smokeless society and nothing less will do.

THE RESPONSE OF INTEREST GROUPS DURING
THE THIRD WAVE OF REGULATION

Among the results of the controversy surrounding the passive smoking issue has been a dramatic increase in the number of legislative
proposals regulating smoking in public places or proposing increases
in cigarette excise taxes (see Figures 2.2 and 2.3). One of the factors that
has made this Third Wave of regulation unique is the new interest
shown by state and local governments in regulating the cigarette industry. Legislation that involves restrictions on smoking in various public
places has been much more severe at the local and state level than at the
federal level. This burst of legislative activity has not been confined to
just the state and local levels of government. Figure 2.3 illustrates that
congressional interest in the smoking and health issue has increased
fourfold since 1986.

Neither does it appear that the furor surrounding the smoking and
health issue is subsiding. A survey of major news publications (*Time*,
Newsweek, the *Wall Street Journal*, and the *New York Times* as well as major
newspapers throughout the U.S.) has revealed that the smoking and
health issue and, in particular, the passive smoking issue, has appeared
at least 500 times since January 1988 (*Congressional Budget Office*,
4/14/94). In fact, the topic of passive smoking has been a cover story
on either *Time* or *Newsweek* eight times since 1988. Thus, the controversy
surrounding this issue seems to be intensifying instead of lessening
with the passage of time.

Academic Interest: Economists, Health Care Specialists

How has the academic world reacted to this renewed interest in the
cigarette industry? Not surprisingly, economists have returned to familiar themes from the two previous "waves" of regulation. Economists
are again studying the effects of excise tax increases and advertising
bans on the consumption of cigarettes. An example of this would be a
study conducted by the Congressional Budget Office suggesting that
the elasticity of demand for cigarettes has remained constant at $-.4$ and
$-.5$ (Congressional Budget Office, *The Tobacco Industry*, Spring 1987). In
Chapters 4 and 5, the effects of the various policy measures are investigated by examining the effects these measures had on the cigarette sales
of individual states. Other economists are exploring the topic that was
the chief concern of economists during the First Wave of regulation: the
structure of the cigarette industry. Jeffrey Harris, a medical doctor and
economist at MIT, has made the suggestion that a windfall profits tax
be levied against the earnings of the cigarette firms because of the

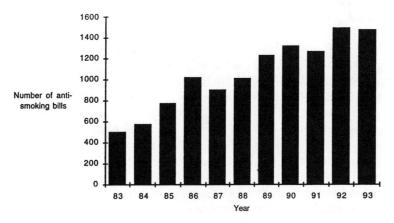

Figure 2.2 State and local legislative activity. *Source: Tobacco Observer* (1983 to 1993)

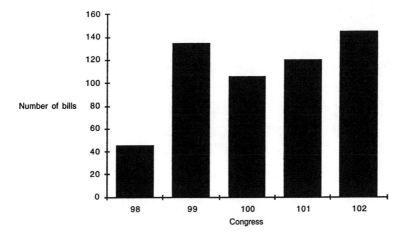

Figure 2.3 Congressional activity. *Source: Tobacco Observer* (1983 to 1993)

oligopolistic nature of the industry (Harris, 1987, p. 24). One example Harris gives that illustrates the oligopolistic nature of this industry is the manner in which cigarette firms deal with cigarette excise tax increases. Harris charges that the price increases for cigarettes far exceed the level justified by the tax increase. In other words, the excise tax increase is an excuse for milking the consumer. Chapter 5 will examine Harris's charge to see if indeed the cigarette firms are behaving in this manner.

Another group that has a stake in this renewed interest in smoking and health is, of course, health care specialists. The chief spokesperson for this group of scholars is Dr. Kenneth Warner, who has been teaching at the University of Michigan's Public Health Institute since 1984 and has been secretary for the Council on Smoking Prevention since 1985. Warner has written extensively (at least fourteen articles on smoking and health since 1979) on almost every aspect of smoking prevention and has advocated all of the various measure that are thought to decrease cigarette smoking, including advertising bans, smoking bans, and excise tax increases. In his articles, Warner's arguments combine an interesting blend of medical research about the effects of cigarette smoking on the health of individuals with empirical results about the effectiveness of policy measures designed to discourage cigarette smoking. Besides the "traditional" antismoking measures, Warner and his fellow health care scholars have also advocated some more radical solutions to the smoking and health problem. Examples of these radical proposals would be nationalization of the cigarette industry, total abolition of the price support system for tobacco (Warner, 1985, p. 348), and a 15 percent tax on cigarette profits to be used to finance antismoking advertisements (Tye, 1986, p. 23). Once again, it is apparent that passive smoking has given new life to an old issue, smoking and health, and enabled the antismoking forces to go on the offensive in order to achieve their goal of a smoke-free society.

THE CIGARETTE INDUSTRY'S RESPONSE TO THE THIRD WAVE OF REGULATION

The reaction of the cigarette industry to the dramatic increase of government interference in the cigarette industry was to intensify the developments already taking place as a result of the Second Wave of regulation. But there were significant differences. We will see that the amount and type of diversification activity which has taken place since the inception of the Third Wave of regulation is quite different than that which occurred in the Second Wave. The trend toward "internationalization" becomes much more significant. Finally, a majority of the firms were simply faced with the question of when and how to exit the industry. Once again, we will proceed by examining the strategies of each firm in dealing with this Third Wave of regulation.

Philip Morris

Food. During this Third Wave of regulation, PM's corporate strategy appears to be the same as the strategy it employed throughout the

Second Wave. But there have been significant changes. The first one is the type of firm that PM has begun to acquire and the amount PM is willing to pay for these acquisitions. With the purchase of Kraft in 1988, Philip Morris became the largest food packager in the United States as well as the tenth largest corporation on the Fortune 500 list. Operating revenues increased from $31.7 billion in 1988 to $44.8 billion in 1989, and current assets increased by $1.2 billion to a total of $9.3 billion. To pay for Kraft, PM dipped into its cash surplus for $2.7 billion and borrowed $10 billion, which was quite easily paid down using the cash flow from the cigarette operations and cutting costs by finding "synergies" between the Kraft and GF operations. Obviously, observers on Wall Street liked what they observed about this newest addition to the PM family, for PM's stock price climbed by 23 percent in the four months following the purchase.

How did the purchase of Kraft, now known as Kraft General Foods, change the corporate structure of PM? In 1989, PM's food division accounted for 51 percent of operating revenue, cigarettes accounted for 40 percent, and beer for 8 percent. However, cigarettes still accounted for over 72 percent of PM's operating profits, with the food division contributing 22 percent and beer adding 3 percent. Certainly, PM had become much larger but whether this size was correlated with much larger profits seems doubtful.

But Philip Morris was hardly finished with the building of its food empire. On June 22, 1990, Philip Morris bought the world's second largest coffee and candy producer, Jacobs Suchard A.G. of Zurich, for $3.8 billion. What effect the purchase of Suchard will have on Philip Morris's performance in the future remains to be seen. But this purchase did have two immediate effects. In terms of its diversification strategy, Philip Morris has acquired a firm that has an entrenched and strong presence in the European food marketplace and quite a healthy cash flow of nearly $1 billion for 1989. Acquiring a position in the European marketplace had been a major concern of PM for quite some time. Finally, with this acquisition, PM has become the largest food processing company in the world and the fifth largest corporation in the United States. What further acquisitions PM will make in the future has been the focus of much speculation in the financial press, but it does appear that PM's criteria for acquisitions has changed. No longer does PM appear to be employing the "puffer belly" strategy (i.e., growth for growth's sake). Kraft General Foods and Suchard were both highly profitable firms. However, both of these firms realized that if they were going to compete with other food giants in the future, they would need additional sources of revenue for future product development. This is a role that PM could certainly fulfill. Yet PM was not willing to pay the "premium" for these acquisitions. No longer would PM pay 3.75 times the stock price of the firm as it did when it purchased Miller Beer and General Foods. Because of its enormous size, PM's management no longer had to fear a leveraged buyout attempt. Instead, management seemed to be adding acquisitions that were able to add even more cash flow to the bottom line for even more acquisitions, particularly in the international cigarette market.

Tobacco. PM's performance in the U.S. cigarette market has been steady, as can be seen in Figure 2.4. With the rise of generic and discount brands of cigarettes, PM found it necessary to reduce the retail price of Marlboro (which alone accounts for 23.5 percent of the total U.S. market share) to increase market share and fight off further inroads by the generic brands. With this price cut, PM managed to increase its market share by 1.1 percent and earned a pretax average of 30 cents on every pack of cigarettes it sells in the United States. Thus, after twenty five years of diversification activity, domestic cigarette revenue still accounts for nearly one third of its operating income. See Table 2.7 for a complete breakdown of PM's business segments.

Philip Morris International is the leading U.S. exporter of cigarettes, exporting $18.4 billion worth of cigarettes in 1994. PM International has nearly tripled its international cigarettes sales since the start of the Third Wave of regulation (*Philip Morris Annual Report 1993*, p. 5). World

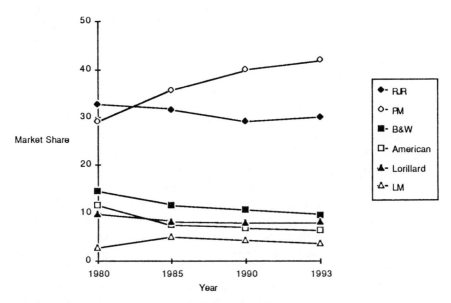

Figure 2.4 American cigarette industry (1980 to 1993). *Source: Business Week* (1980 to 1993)

Table 2.7 PM's various business segments during the Third Wave.
Source: Philip Morris Inc. Annual Report (1993), p. 1.

Operating Revenue (in billions)	1993	1992	1991
Tobacco (Domestic & International)	25.97	25.68	23.84
Food (Domestic & International)	30.37	29.05	28.18

Operating Profits (in billions)	1993	1992	1991
Tobacco (Domestic & International)	4.91	7.19	6.46
Food (Domestic & International)	2.61	2.77	2.02

Operating Revenue (%)	1993	1992	1991
Tobacco (Domestic & International)	46	47	46
Food (Domestic & International)	54	53	54

Operating Profits (%)	1993	1992	1991
Tobacco (Domestic & International)	65	72	76
Food (Domestic & International)	35	28	24

cigarette industry unit sales (excluding the United States) were approximately 5 trillion in 1993, and Philip Morris International's share of the world market in 1993 was 9.2 percent compared to 8.6 percent in 1992 (Tobacco Institute, *The Economic Contributions of Tobacco*, p. 5). PM International has cigarette market share of at least 15 percent in at least twenty-five countries including Australia, the Federal Republic of Germany, Finland, France, Hong Kong, Italy, Mexico, Saudi Arabia, and Switzerland. It has also acquired businesses in Hungary, the Czech Republic, Lithuania, Russia, and Kazakhstan. PM International has also signed a "cooperation agreement" with the China National Tobacco Corp. However prices in many of Philip Morris International's markets are government controlled. PM also faces higher excise taxes and production costs in these foreign markets, resulting in lower operating margins (only 11.5 cents per pack) and profits as compared to U.S. cigarette sales. So while the international market is increasing, it doesn't provide the ultimate solution to the shrinking U.S. market. Still, PM has far outshone its other U.S. competitors (particularly RJR) in the international cigarette business.

One of the more interesting battles that will continue to face PM's management is the possibility of a spin-off of the tobacco operations from the food operations. It was more than symbolic that when PM's chairman and CEO, Michael A. Miles, who was a former Kraft employee, attempted to split off the tobacco and food operations, he was defeated by forces led by the former chairman, Hamish Maxwell. This defeat led to Mr. Miles's resignation and to the installation of two "tobacco" men, R. William Murray and Geoffrey C. Bible, as chairman and CEO, respectively. To mollify institutional investors, who were quite eagerly anticipating rather hefty profits from the spin-off sales, a stock buyback proposal worth $3 billion was proposed to raise the price of PM stock (Business Week, 7/4/94, pp. 26–27). Hence, it appears that the PM empire will still be intact as it enters the twenty-first century. The strategy of protecting the tobacco business while using tobacco profits to further the food business and other tobacco acquisitions appears to be the direction PM will follow for the foreseeable future.

RJR Nabisco

As we have just seen, RJR's archrival PM had stayed the course of its "puffer belly" strategy. While the result of this persistence might not have been in the greatest interest of PM's shareholders, it did produce a corporate colossus capable of producing a cash flow of nearly $11 billion.

However, in October 1988, the top management of RJR, particularly F. Ross Johnson, was losing patience with RJR's puffer belly strategy. Johnson saw an opportunity to begin a leveraged buyout (LBO) attempt and to become an extremely rich man if he could pull off this buyout. But his attempt was foiled by Kohlberg, Kravis, Roberts (KKR) and the story was immortalized in the book *Barbarians at the Gate*. But for our purposes the real significance of this attempted LBO was that it left RJR Nabisco a much weaker firm. Its ability to compete with its archrival PM was greatly diminished and as a result it became much more dependent on its tobacco segment to produce the income it needed to pay off the tremendous amounts of debt (still $13.9 billion six years after the takeover) that KKR had incurred to buy RJR Nabisco. Hence, RJR Nabisco entered the Third Wave of regulation in a greatly weakened condition that made it much more desperate to defend its lucrative tobacco segment.

Tobacco. RJR has lost market share fairly consistently throughout the Third Wave of regulation, as can be seen in Figure 2.4. To defend its market share, RJR began to develop much more aggressive advertising campaigns, Joe Camel being the symbol of these controversial campaigns. Joe Camel has become a target for antismoking forces, which view the friendly dromedary as a ploy to market cigarettes to children rather than adults. RJR vehemently denies the antismoking groups' allegations of enticing the young to smoke. It certainly appears that RJR is in the U.S. cigarette business to stay and is quite willing to take on the antismoking forces. RJR also had to match the cut in prices which PM enacted in 1993.

Tobacco International (RJR's international tobacco subsidiary) markets its products in all major international markets. Sales are accomplished through exports from the United States, from foreign manufacturing operations, and through license agreements with foreign governments. Key markets in which manufacturing subsidiaries are located include Belgium, Brazil, Canada, Ecuador, Malaysia, Puerto Rico, Switzerland, and West Germany. Imports from the United States are promoted in Hong Kong, France, Spain, and Singapore (*RJR Nabisco Annual Report 1993*, p. 23). RJR's international operations in 1993 were approximately one third the size of PM International. Clearly, PM is besting RJR both on the domestic and international cigarette fronts.

Food. Even with the large amount of debt foisted on RJR by KKR, Nabisco has still managed to remain the largest manufacturer and marketer of cookies and crackers in the United States. But even with holding its preeminence in its traditional markets, the vast majority of RJR profits are still tobacco related. Like its chief competitor, it has seen a movement to force management to spin off the tobacco operations from the food operations. The rationale for the spilt is simple: food firms are valued at 18.4 times earnings whereas tobacco firms are at 8.4 times earnings. Therefore, it seems that the tobacco segment of RJR is dragging down its food stock. However, the real problem with this separation is the amount of debt ($13.9 billion) with which the KKR buyout saddled the company. Obviously, one would like to put most of the debt on the tobacco firm since its huge cash flows and profit margins would enable it to pay off the debt much easier. But bondholders might balk at such an arrangement given that the tobacco business is under legal fire (*Business Week*, 8/30/93, p. 58).

KKR had also proposed to take over Borden by using its equity position in RJR. It would pay for Borden by sharply reducing KKR's equity holdings from 35 percent of RJR to 17.5 percent, a transaction worth $2 billion. Since 1989, KKR has reduced its equity holdings in RJR from 100 percent of RJR Nabisco, which cost KKR $25 billion. It seems that KKR wanted to reduce its exposure to possible tobacco

Table 2.8   RJR's various business segments during the third wave.
Source: RJR Nabisco Annual Report (1993), p. 3.

Operating Revenue (in billions)	1993	1992	1991
Tobacco	8.08	9.03	8.54
Food	7.03	6.71	6.45

Operating Profits(in billions)	1993	1992	1991
Tobacco	.89	2.24	2.32
Food	.62	.77	.72

Operating Revenue(%)	1993	1992	1991
Tobacco	53	57	57
Food	47	43	43

Operating Profits(%)	1993	1992	1991
Tobacco	65	74	75
Food	35	26	25

liability suits and was willing to take a risk that it could develop Borden's well-established but troubled brands. However, this plan eventually fell through, although KKR still intended to purchase Borden but without using its RJR stock as leverage. This whole incident was certainly not a strong vote of confidence by KKR in RJR Nabisco's future prospects (*New York Times*, September 13, 1994, pp. D1, D5).

In this continuing effort to free itself from the tobacco industry, RJR announced it would give investors a chance to buy a stake in its Nabisco holdings alone. These stockholders would be able to stay clear of the tobacco interests. RJR planned to sell $1 billion worth of this nontobacco stock to retire its $10 billion in bank debt (*Boston Herald*, November 1, 1994, p. 33).

Once again, we are witnessing how the market continues to put pressure on these food-tobacco companies to split their divisions. However, we have also seen how forsaking the lucrative tobacco business is extremely difficult. In many ways, PM and RJR have become addicted to tobacco just as much as any of their customers. See Figure 2.8.

The Little Four: Brown and Williamson,
Lorillard, L&M, American

Going into the Third Wave of regulation, the position of the "little four" of the U.S. cigarette industry was at best precarious. These firms were left to fight among themselves for what market share PM and RJR left them. With the coming of the Third Wave of regulation, the pressure to exit this industry became even more intense. Hence, these firms were faced with the following sets of questions: 1. Should they remain in the cigarette business and "harvest" the still substantial cash flows which cigarette operations can produce? 2. Should they "exit" the industry and how should they time the exit so as to maximize the price that they can receive for their cigarette operations? We will now examine how these firms reacted to these questions.

L&M became the first firm to make a move in reaction to the threats of the coming of the Third Wave of regulation. In 1986, Grand Met sold off L&M's tobacco division to Bennett S. LeBow, a New York investor, in a highly leveraged buyout deal. Besides changing the firm's name from L&M to the Ligget Group, Mr. LeBow changed Ligget's business strategy. Ligget became the largest producer of "generic" cigarettes while sacrificing its own premium brands. Ligget did pick up some market share when it employed this strategy, but the profits were considerably less than those of other cigarette producers. As we have seen earlier, PM responded to this generic threat by cutting its prices on its premium brands and immediately recovered the market share it had lost to this generic strategy. Thus, the future of the highly leveraged Liggett group, with its slumping market share and reliance on slimmer-margin generic cigarettes, is at best bleak.

One of the characteristics of the Third Wave has been the emphasis by PM and RJR on being much more aggressive in acquiring additional foreign outlets for their products. Obviously, foreign competitors are also quite interested in entering the still-lucrative U.S. cigarette market. Lorillard would appear the most likely target of foreign interest. Lorillard still possesses a highly successful brand (Newport). Certainly, Lorillard's owner, the Loews Group, would be interested in shedding that brand it if it needed to raise cash in order to acquire to supplement its CBS holdings. Lorillard continues to be a source of needed revenue for the Loews Corporation and its owner, Lawrence Tisch. However, there is little doubt that Tisch would sell Lorillard if the bid was right, especially from a foreign cigarette manufacturer who might be tempted to pay a premium price to gain access to the U.S. cigarette market (*Business Week*, May 16, 1994, p. 126).

Brown and Williamson, the largest of the "little four," decided it needed to pick up additional market share if it was going to remain a viable force in the U.S. cigarette industry. Its purchase of American Tobacco for $1 billion (at nine times earnings) allowed Brown and Williamson to pick up a 6.7 percent market share and increase its overall market share to 18 percent of the cigarette market. With this purchase, it appears that BAT, the British parent company of Brown and Williamson, is not ready to concede the U.S. cigarette market to PM and RJR. With this proposed purchase of American Tobacco, BAT hopes to keep PM and RJR busy on the home front so that BAT might have some room to operate its traditional foreign (primarily European and Asian) markets (*The Economist*, April 30, 1994, p. 75).

However, the U.S. Justice Department announced that it would oppose this merger. The rationale used by the Justice Department was that this merger would limit competition in the U.S. cigarette industry. Needless to say, there will be a protracted court battle over this proposed merger (*New York Times*, November 2, 1994, D.1). The question that bought about the First Wave of regulation of the cigarette industry seems to have reappeared during the Third Wave.

Overall, the Third Wave of regulation of the cigarette industry appears to have continued the trend toward consolidation in the cigarette industry begun in the Second Wave of regulation. In many ways, the cigarette industry now appears to resemble the U.S. soft drink industry. There are two giants firms that dominate the domestic market and are fighting fiercely to gain control over foreign markets, with the U.S. government occasionally making attempts to stimulate competition in the U.S. market. Ironically, the chief difference between the cigarette and soft drink industries is the size of their market, the cigarette market being worth five times that of the soft drink industry.

SUMMARY

This chapter has discussed the three waves of regulation that have occurred during the one-hundred-year existence of the cigarette industry. During the First Wave of regulation, the federal government was primarily concerned with the structure of the cigarette industry. The Duke Trust had a monopoly on most tobacco products and so the American Tobacco Co. was broken up into a tightly knit oligopoly.

The Second Wave of regulation was a result of the public's concern over the smoking and health issue. This issue had a profound effect on the strategies of the cigarette firms both at the business level (market segmentation, international markets) and at the corporate level (diversification). The smoking and health issue also resulted in an antismoking movement whose primary aim was reduced cigarette smoking. Thus, the actions (advertising bans, smoking bans, and excise tax increases) that government took during this period had as their goal to discourage smoking. Yet we have seen how the smoking and health issue also had a profound effect on the structure of the cigarette industry. At the start of the Second Wave, the industry was led by two firms (RJR and American) that had almost 58 percent of the market while the other four firms split the rest of the market equally. At the conclusion of the Second Wave, the structure of the industry had radically changed. Two firms, Philip Morris and RJR, had almost 74 percent of the market while the other four firms grabbed for the remaining market. In essence, a duopoly had developed as a result of this new round of regulation.

With the advent of the "passive" smoking or secondhand smoking issue, a Third Wave of regulation was foisted upon the U.S. cigarette industry. Antismoking advocates became much more zealous in their pursuit of the cigarette industry, and public opinion in general turned against not only the industry but its consumers. With this Third Wave of regulation, the cigarette industry is facing opponents at all levels of government whose goal is to virtually destroy the industry and who are no longer willing to compromise about what they perceive to be the evils of cigarette smoking.

This Third Wave of regulation also intensified some of the trends that were developing during the two previous waves of regulation. The corporate strategies of the cigarette firms were still focused on the goal of diversification. However, for the two largest cigarette firms, PM and RJR, this diversification included grabbing significant portions of the international cigarette market. The structure of the cigarette industry became even more concentrated with the likely exit of many of the smaller firms.

Thus, the cigarette industry and its relationship to the various stakeholders that are interested in it presents a complex but fascinating problem to students of both the business and public policy processes. Various public policy measures affect both the strategies of the cigarette firms and the structure of the cigarette industry. But the cigarette industry, with its considerable contribution to the economy, can also influence the manner in which government deals with these calls for regulation. In the next chapter, I propose a model that hopes to encompass not only all of the groups concerned with the cigarette industry but also the policy processes that shape both the strategies of the cigarette firms and structure of the cigarette industry. The cigarette industry is at a critical time in its history. Although sales increased slightly in 1994, this increase had been preceded by a decline in sales of 1.2 percent per year since 1984. However, all through this period, the industry's profits averaged an all-time high of a little over $6 billion, with pretax margins approaching 30 percent. Margins on foreign cigarette sales averaged a mere 5 percent so that the foreign sales have not become the ultimate solution to the cigarette firms' problem. For PM and RJR, the vast majority of profits still come from domestic cigarette sales. Meanwhile, the smaller cigarette firms are faced with the question of whether to exit the industry or combine with other smaller cigarette makers to maintain market presence. But one thing is certain for the foreseeable future: the 55 million Americans who smoke cigarettes will be able to purchase their favorite American brands with little difficulty since both the cigarette firms and the government are unable to leave them empty-handed.

3

A Convergence Model for Business and Public Policy

INTRODUCTION

In Chapter 2, it was shown that the cigarette industry has undergone three distinct but related waves of regulation throughout its history. The driving force behind the First Wave of public policy measures aimed at the cigarette industry was the public's reaction to the industry's pricing policies resulting from the oligopolistic structure of the industry. Even though the U.S. government initiated and won antitrust suits in 1913 and 1941, the public outcry against the cigarette industry's pricing policy has never really been settled. Neither of these governmental interventions dealt effectively with the two fundamental issues that affect the structure of this industry: the economies of scale needed to produce cigarettes efficiently and the cost of national advertising needed to promote individual brands.

With the Second Wave of regulation, the health issue was raised against the cigarette industry by the evidence linking cigarette smoking to cancer, emphysema, and heart disease. But while the chief objection of the antismoking forces had changed during the Second Wave, they were never able to ignore the issue that had initiated the First Wave, namely, the structure of the cigarette industry. Economic power meant political power. Hence, by the end of the Second Wave of regulation, there were two issues that were part of the public agenda facing the cigarette industry: the structure of the industry and the power derived from it, and the public harm from smoking as seen in the health issue.

Once again, it was the federal government that initiated various policy measures such as warning labels and advertising bans to deal with the public's new concern. The aim of these measures was to reduce the level of cigarette sales. The success of these measures on cigarette consumption will be analyzed in Chapter 4. The record clearly indicates that these measures were undertaken as part of a political compromise.

While the cigarette industry objected vehemently to warning labels and the TV and radio cigarette advertising ban, these measures were merely a preview of the much stronger measures that would be undertaken during the Third Wave of regulation.

With emergence of the passive smoking issue, the current Third Wave of regulation emerged. Public policy measures such as restrictions on smoking in various public places and stiff excise tax increases seem to be the favorite methods of a much more vocal antismoking movement. Even though cigarette sales were declining in the early 1980s at the end of the Second Wave, this decline was far too little and was taking far too long to satisfy the antismoking forces.

But opponents of the cigarette industry now had a new phrase to add to the antismoking arsenal: the "rights of the nonsmoker." New measures seek to decrease not only cigarette smoking but to protect nonsmokers from cigarette smoke. These measures are much more radical than those proposed in earlier times. Yet these measures still reflect concerns from the previous waves: a call to nationalize the cigarette industry can be linked to the structure and power issue; a total cigarette advertising ban and the enactment of the very high excise tax rates are being proposed in order to decrease cigarette sales; smoking prohibition laws are aimed at protecting the "rights of the nonsmoker."

Several points can be made about the cigarette industry's relationship with its external environment. First, no "issue" was ever completely settled by public policy makers during the course of a wave or a succeeding wave. While there were attempts made by public policy makers to deal with the various "driving forces," none of these issues was even remotely settled.

Second, each succeeding wave of regulation was reinforced by the driving force of previous waves. Thus, when the cigarette industry faced the Third Wave of regulation, the passive smoking controversy revitalized the smoking and health issue and rekindled the interest of economists and critics in studying the structure of the cigarette industry and its political power. Figure 3.1 is a graphic representation of what the life cycle for policy issues looks like for the cigarette industry (Post, 1978, p. 21). Any model that hopes to capture the relationship between the cigarette industry and its external environment must be able to capture three different processes involved in the cigarette smoking "issue set." First, the model must be able to account for the cumulative nature of the issues that face the cigarette industry. Since the early 1900s, the cigarette industry and government policy makers have never faced just a single issue but many issues (which I will hereinafter refer to as an issue set.) As more and more issues are added to this set, more and more opponents are arrayed against the industry involved. The force

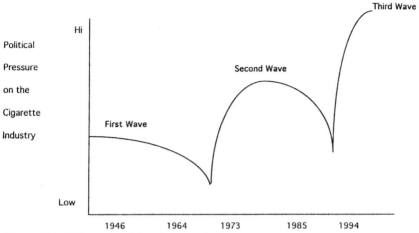

Figure 3.1 Life cycle of the cigarette industry-government issue set.

that molds these various issues into a coherent set is "ideology." It is the contention of many scholars that an "ideology of antismoking" has developed since 1985 (Berger, 1986, p. 234). The model needs to account for the factors that need to be present for this ideology to form and what role that ideology plays in forming the issue set. The issue set is not static but influences two other dynamic processes: public policy and business policy. It is these two decision-making processes that will make up the two parts of any proposed model of business and government relations.

There are many questions that decision makers in the public policy process face as they are confronted with an issue set. What forum or branch of government will be chosen by the advocates of an issue set? At what level of government (federal, state, or local) will the issue set be presented? What sorts of governmental measures or interventions are being proposed by the various groups involved in the issue set?

Business policy makers are confronted with questions similar to those that confront public policy makers. Should the issue set be addressed by the firm or is it an industry question? Should the firm/industry deal with the issues at the national, regional, or state level? How will the proposed public policy measures or interventions affect the structure of the industry or the strategies of the firms in the industry?

The present challenges to the legitimacy of the cigarette industry include but also go beyond the competitive and political forces of earlier times. To understand the challenges and demands on both public and business policy makers and make it possible to assess the effects of policy interventions, it is necessary to develop a model that can include all of the above stakeholders with their diverse political, economic, and ideological views and the complex institutional forces that shape business, government, and society.

A CONVERGENCE MODEL FOR BUSINESS AND PUBLIC POLICY

The foundation for the model (see Figure 3.2) proposed in this chapter comes from two separate but related sources in the Social Issues in Management field: the "interpenetrating systems" approach to issue management as developed by Preston and Post (1975), and the stakeholder approach advocated by Freeman (1984).

The "interpenetrating systems" approach to issue management allows a researcher to answer two questions: 1. How are the various groups related? 2. What sort of sequence or "timing" is necessary for an issue set to develop? To answer the first question, the "interpenetrating systems approach" utilizes a concept from set theory called intersection. Intersection is an operation that illustrates what two or more groups have in common. This "intersection" concept accounts for the phenomenon whereby diverse groups that seemingly have very little in common are drawn into a coalition when a public policy issue is expanded sufficiently. The second question concerning the sequence or timing of events can be dealt with using a stage theory approach to issue management. Systems analysis can be thought of as an evolutionary process in which a policy issue must "mature" or go through certain phases over time. For example, see Post (1978, p. 22), and Mahon (1983, 1994). While this concept has great intuitive appeal, the model must be able to accommodate the various choices that decision makers have to make as an "issue set" goes through the various decision-making processes.

The interpenetrating systems model proposes that stakeholders have two choices when they select a forum for advocacy: they can determine what level of government (local, state, or federal) is appropriate and also what branch of government (executive, judicial, or legislative) is desirable. A comparable phenomenon occurs in the business decision process as well. A public policy issue can be dealt with at either the firm or industry level, and various parts of the organization will be called upon to deal with an issue at various points of time.

Stakeholder analysis involves the analysis of all the major groups involved in any public policy or corporate policy decision. But it is not enough merely to list which groups are interested in a particular issue or controversy. The researcher must measure or account for the intensity or commitment each of these interest groups brings to an issue. One

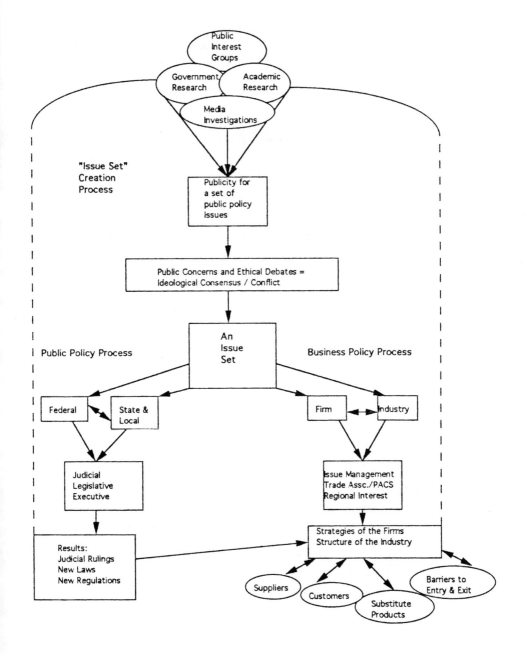

Figure 3.2 A convergence model of business and public policy.

could measure this factor by the amount of funds devoted to an issue, the number of members in the stakeholder groups, or the amount of attention paid to a controversial issue by a CEO or public relations department. Finally, stakeholder analysis is inadequate unless it includes both the political and the economic power that a group can bring to a public or business policy decision. Obviously, these two factors are related but they do not necessarily coincide, for it truly depends on the nature of the issue and the commitment that a group has to make if it wants to deal with an issue.

The Convergence Model will have three parts in order to accommodate the preceding concerns : the "issue set" creation process, the public policy process, and the business policy process. The model demonstrates how these three distinct processes affect each other in determining the eventual resolution of any business-societal concern.

As applied to the cigarette industry, the model deals with the concept of ideology and how it is the catalyst for the creation of an issue set that is the driving force behind the passive smoking issue. The various parts of the public policy process will be analyzed in the second part, and the business policy process will be the subject of study for the third section of the model. As was mentioned earlier, most of these "parts" or sections have components that will utilize models or schema currently found in Social Issues and Business Policy literature. As each part of the model is examined, two areas will be addressed: first, there will be a review of the literature from which that part of the model was developed; and second, an explanation will be given of how and why the various components of the "part" fit together.

PART 1—THE "ISSUE SET" CREATION PROCESS

The concept of the issue set was first proposed by Donna Woods (Woods, 1986, p. 37). In her description of the food industry, she points out that the 1906 Pure Food Act was not the result of a public outcry but rather the result of a chain of events that was "complex and lengthy" (ibid., p. 8). The bill was passed only after Congress had considered no fewer than "56 pure food bills" over a sixteen-year period (ibid., p. 9). The 1906 Pure Food Act was therefore a compromise bill that all of the groups concerned with pure food could support. But this solution satisfied no one group completely and was made possible because all of the parties had been able to reach what appears to have been an "ideological consensus."

Ideology is a term often associated with extremes. Right-wing or left-wing ideologues are characterized as people who will either trample on the rights of others to further their cause (right-wing ideologues) or fail to take into account the various costs to society in implementing the "correct" solution (left-wing ideologues). In either case, the end justifies the means. At first glance, the notion of an "ideological consensus" sounds like an oxymoron.

However, the concept of ideology can be put forth in a much more positive light (Lodge, 1986, p. 62). It can be looked at as a study of assumptions, specifically, ethical assumptions. These assumptions are a result of the two traditional sources of ethical reasoning: teleological (end results) and deontological (rights of individuals). The ideology that revolves around any issue set is very much a product of the type of ethical reasoning used to establish or defend a group's position on a particular issue set. Some groups will employ an ideology that promises something for everyone (utilitarianism) while others will employ an ideology based on "right" principles (ideology of rights). Recalling Figure 3.1, one could make a case that the ideology of utilitarianism was employed in the first two waves of the cigarette public policy life cycle whereas an ideology of rights characterizes the Third Wave. This pattern of ideological development also seems to hold even with such diverse issue sets as civil rights, the oil industry, alcohol, and gambling. Hence, ideologies of rights seem to be employed much later in the life cycle of an issue set whereas ideologies resulting from a utilitarian mode of thinking characterize the early debate in the life cycle of an issue set. But whatever type of ideology is chosen it is the result of an ethical consensus or compromise reached by the various groups involved in the issue set.

Establishment groups may have as one of their goals the preservation of the status quo. This can be viewed as the willingness to compromise (accommodation) or to sell out (appeasement). To achieve this compromise, establishment groups generally use utilitarian or cost-benefit analysis types of reasoning when they present their case in the public arena. The correct action is the one that produces the greatest good with the least amount of controversy. Thus, these establishment groups employ an ideology of utilitarianism. No one leaves the political process empty-handed; the political pie is expanded and all sides leave the table somewhat satisfied with the status quo still intact.

Meanwhile, the concerns of single-interest groups such as STAT, GASP, MADD (Mothers Against Drunk Driving), and NOW are by their very nature much more normative. An action or a cause is either right or wrong. There is little or no room for compromise. The concept of cost or keeping the status quo intact is not a concern for these groups. The "right" solution should be enacted regardless of the costs.

Hence, single-interest groups may employ an ideology of rights. The political process for single-interest groups is a zero-sum game and the winner takes all. Even if these groups are forced to compromise, they will want to press the political process again when they ascertain that more of the political pie can be gained at the expense of their adversaries. But this is also the reason why this confrontational ideology becomes the consensus ideology later in the life cycle of an issue set.

Yet, as the pure food controversy illustrates, the public policy process will only begin when both establishment and single-issue groups have some ground on which they can reconcile their ethical (ideological) assumptions. It is at this point that a policy action can be justified on both utilitarian and normative grounds. One of these ethical arguments might predominate depending on how the issue is brought before the public agenda (newspapers, academic journals, or other sources) and what ethical arguments are used to support the various positions on the issue. Then there is a power struggle between establishment groups and single-issue groups as to whose position will be "representative" for the issue set. Both groups make appeals for public support and either a political compromise or a conflict will develop. Establishment groups hope to satisfy enough people to lay the issue at rest while single-issue groups hope to achieve total victory. The result of all of this political maneuvering is an issue set that might have broad appeal to many groups (compromise) or very specific appeal to a majority of the population (conflict). But, in any event, some sort of consensus concerning the public attitude toward an issue set is reached.

Public policy makers generally prefer a consensus issue. In this type of situation, a legislator will not have to alienate any part of her/his constituency. Obviously, at times, a representative or a senator will have to champion a "conflict" piece of legislation that will put that legislator at odds with fellow legislators. It is at these times where the political process can become quite complex.

For business policy makers, the formation of an issue set is a time of both great opportunity and risk. If the issue set is one of conflict that will negatively affect its business or industry, does the business policy maker try to portray the "zealots" (single-issue groups) as the true representatives of the issue set, for example, Philip Morris's strategy on smoking and health (*Business Week*, 7/4/94, p. 62) or does the business policy maker back establishment groups in the hope that these groups can moderate any adverse public policy actions? Such questions and process issues run throughout the controversy surrounding cigarettes and the passive smoking issue.

PART 2—THE PUBLIC POLICY PROCESS

There are a number of models that describe the public policy process, some of which include: Preston and Post (1975), Dye (1978), and Carroll (1993). Although these models do not capture this complex process completely, they are certainly adequate to describe the key features of this process. However, these models do have different emphases: some stress all the various stages public policy measures must traverse in order to be enacted (comprehensiveness); others focus more on the dynamics (i.e., what is going on during each stage) of the decision-making process rather than listing all the necessary stages.

Both of these elements—comprehensiveness and dynamic interactions—are valuable to have in any model describing the public policy process. Yet one of these features is often compromised to highlight the other. The present model includes both elements, but it is more concerned that the dynamic elements be preserved to concentrate on answering questions about the effectiveness of various policy interventions.

One model that stresses the dynamic qualities of the public policy process is the interpenetrating systems model of Preston and Post (1978, p. 22). This model is dynamic because it takes into account the timing element, which is a crucial element not only to the formation of an issue set but to understand the impact of interventions on business and public policy. In keeping with this "interpenetrating systems" tradition, the Convergence of Business and Public Policy model will also stress the "timing" of interventions and the effects these interventions have on business and public policy. In the public policy process, there will be several "timing" and "interventions" questions:

> At what level of government do the advocates of an "issue set" want to present their case ?
>
> To what branch of government do they want to make their first appeal?
>
> What objectives or goals are the advocates of government interventions trying to achieve?
>
> What measures are being advocated to achieve these goals?
>
> How will it be determined if these goals are being met; are there unintended effects these measures are having on the structure of an industry or the strategies of firms?

The Civil Rights movement in the 1960s provides an excellent example of the dynamic nature of the public policy process. Civil Rights groups first used the federal courts to address racial injustices. After these groups were successful and gained some power, they next moved to Congress to further the movement's cause. Then the civil rights groups appealed to individual state legislatures to initiate even more interventions. The process is continuous and appeals are continuously made not only to different branches of the government but also to the different levels of government.

Likewise, there are issues that can start at the state level and move up to the federal level, such as Prohibition. In another respect, the Prohibition issue was also interesting in that it is an example of an issue that had a "regional" aspect to it, because it was championed in the southern part of the country. In the case of the antismoking issue, the procigarette cause receives support from the Southeast congressional delegation, and the antismoking forces seems to derive its strength from the Northeast and West Coast delegations.

There are numerous other policy instruments that can emanate either from the executive or the legislative branches. Economic incentives such as subsidies, quotas, and tax breaks are enacted either to help a struggling industry (agriculture, automobiles) or to spur development in others (oil, solar power). Regulatory agencies are set up to supervise the activities of industries ranging from communication (FCC) to aviation (FAA). If Congress and the president want to have a more direct hand in affecting the policy or conduct of an industry, measures can be employed that have a direct impact on the consumption of a good or service. Examples of this type of action are excise tax increases, bans, and outright prohibition of a good or service.

Obviously, whatever type of measure is taken depends largely on at what branch and at what level of government the issue set is presented. But the public policy process does not end here. The impact of these measures has to be determined or somehow estimated. The impact of a policy includes the short-term effect on the target group or industry; the effect on the other groups involved in the issue set; and the indirect costs to all groups in the long run (Dye, 1978, p. 312).

Whether a policy is thought to be "successful" largely determines if the business-public policy process will conclude. "Success" can sometimes be measured but at other times it is merely symbolic (Edelman, 1964). Even if a measure is thought to be successful in achieving its public policy objectives, an issue set is always capable of being activated from outside sources, including the newsmedia or by various research foundations. For this reason, there is a broken line at the conclusion of both the public and business processes. These lines indicate that the "system" under which these processes operate is a continuous one and is capable of being renewed at any time.

Yet, as legislation or judicial rulings are being implemented, the parties that will be affected do not stand idly. They, too, will react to an issue set and will try to affect the outcome of the public policy process at one level and in turn be affected by the outcome of the public policy process at another level. In this model, that other party is the business policy process, which is the final part of the Convergence Model to be examined.

PART 3—THE BUSINESS POLICY PROCESS

Once again, there exist many models that do an excellent job of describing the business policy process. An example of a business policy model that utilizes, in a parsimonious manner, the literature on this subject is the model developed by Fahey and Narayanan (1986, p. 190). There are two reason why this model is attractive. First, this model emphasizes the levels of environment (task, competitive, and macro) on which an issue set can be presented to the business policy process (ibid., p. 25). Second, there is also a dynamic element that is a component of this model and involves the following decisions: At what level of the business environment will the issue set have the greatest impact, i.e., firm or industry? What sort of organizational "setup" will be the primary spokesperson for the firm/industry as it deals with an issue set in beginning its journey through the public policy process?

In dealing with the second question, three choices are available to a firm or industry: If a firm must deal with the issue set, should it develop its own "in-house" expertise? If it is an industry question, should it form a PAC/Trade association? If the issue is of a regional nature, should a "compact" be developed between the businesses of a region?

The final section of the business policy process evaluates what changes have occurred in the strategies of the firms and the structure of an industry as a result of the business-public policy process. First, it acknowledges the traditional forces that Porter has shown have a profound impact on the strategy of firms and the structure of an industry (Porter, 1980).

The power of customers to affect the strategy of firms and the structure of an industry is traditionally measured by their reaction to price changes in a product. If they buy less of the product, then that product either has a substitute or the consumers can do with less of the product. In this model, there are two other ways in which customers can react to a price change due to an increase in an excise tax rate: either they acquiesce or protest vigorously to their representatives about the "fairness" of such a tax increase. This stakeholder group can also be influenced by bans and court rulings as well. They can also ignore such interventions, as in the case of Prohibition! Obviously, if customers stop buying a good or service as a result of any public policy measure, they will greatly affect the strategies of the firms and the structure of the industry producing that good or service.

The ability of suppliers to influence the strategies and structure of an industry depends on the number of producers and consumers. In the cigarette industry, the power of suppliers to influence the industry is minimal since there are so many suppliers and few customers. Yet, interestingly enough, the structure of the cigarette industry has never been an issue with the tobacco farmers, whose main political concerns are with continuing the tobacco subsidy and hikes in cigarette taxes. So it appears that if the short-term economic interest of the suppliers and the firms in the industry coincide, a strong political alliance can be formed, and interest in the structure of an industry becomes critical only when short-term economic needs are not being met.

The threat of substitute products refers to the extent to which other products exist that can be substituted for the original product. In traditional models of the business policy process, substitute products are thought to hold down the price of the original product. In this current model, substitute products can play a somewhat different role. Product innovations, which could be considered a substitute for the original product, usually remove political pressure to "clean up" a product, for example, the filter cigarette and unleaded gasoline. But if product innovations cannot be advanced and substitutes from other industries are advanced, then the political power of the original industry is weakened. The oil industry experienced this type of phenomenon when solar power, other fossil fuels, and nuclear power were all offered as possible substitutes for generating electrical power.

Finally, barriers to entry and exit can have a profound impact not only on the strategies of firms and the structure of an industry but on how public policy makers view an industry. In industrial organization literature, high entry barriers exist because of economies of scale, high capital requirements, and inaccessibility of distribution channels, all of which characterize the cigarette industry as well as many other industries. But in the Convergence Model, this characteristic of high entry barriers makes an industry a target for both the issue set and public policy processes. If high entry barriers exists, then public policy makers are faced with two courses of action. First, these barriers can be defended as "natural," as in the case of most utilities (electric, telephone), or in the interest of safety or the common good (trucking, railroad, airlines). Otherwise, antitrust action will be initiated by government to respond to demands from public interest groups that competition be fostered.

Exit barriers also play a unique role in the Convergence Model. If a region of the country has a large economic stake in an industry, such as automobiles and steel in the Midwest, then that industry can anticipate that it will be given incentives by government to keep operating its plant(s). It is usually in the interest of public policy makers to keep the exit barriers for an industry as high as possible. Yet there are cases such as cigarettes in which government gives an industry quite conflicting signals as to whether it wants the industry's continued existence. In general, the goal of public policy makers is to keep entry barriers as low as possible and exit barriers as high as possible although there are exceptions based on the economic importance of that industry to a particular region or section of the country.

The final force, which Porter did not include as one of his five forces but which is prominently included in this model, is government intervention. Measures such as judicial rulings, bans, and tax increases have as their goal either to change the policies of firms in an industry or to change the structure of that industry. The question here is not whether government has the power to effect change; certainly it does. But this merely leads to a host of other questions. First, when is it appropriate for government to interfere with the strategies of firms or the structure of an industry? This question is connected to the issue set creation process. If it is ascertained that an industry should be regulated by government, what type of measures(s) ought the government to undertake? What are the criteria for "success" that can be established for these measures? If the measure(s) have failed to achieve their purpose, was it because the measure(s) weren't applied in sufficient "dosages" or simply that they were the wrong policy tools to apply? These are the questions that students of the business process cannot avoid answering if they wish to explain all the various forces that can affect the strategies of firms and the structure of an industry.

CONCLUSION

The Convergence Model of Business and Public Policy was developed for two reasons: (1) to explain the phenomenon of an industry that has undergone three separate waves of government regulation with each wave of regulation having more intensity than the previous one; and (2) to construct systematically hypotheses about the ability of public policy interventions to affect the strategies of the cigarette firms and the structure of the cigarette industry. Although the cigarette industry was the initial impetus for developing such a model, many other industries, ranging from chemicals to alcohol, have similar relationships with government.

The model combines both the interpenetrating systems approach of Preston and Post and the "stakeholder" technique of Freeman. It is this systems approach that enables the model to have a dynamic quality and shows how all of the various groups are related. The stakeholder technique ensures that the model is comprehensive and inclusive.

The research questions that come from this model will emphasize the effects all the forces and groups in this business-public policy system have on the strategies of firms and the structure of an industry. Particular emphasis will be placed on the power of government to interfere with a firm's strategy and an industry's structure. The ability to measure the success of public policy intervention in this area is vital since the success or failure of these interventions largely determines whether the business and public policy process will once again be reactivated.

The focus of the rest of this book will be to evaluate the effects that governmental measures have had on the cigarette industry. The empirical questions that will be examined in Part 2 will have three themes:

1. First, there will be examination of government's attempts to regulate the cigarette during the Second Wave of regulation. The attempts during the Second Wave were focused on influencing the level of cigarette sales through various nontax measures such warning labels and advertising bans. If the government was successful in this endeavor, it also has the power to alter the structure of the cigarette industry without using its most powerful weapon—the excise tax increase.

2. Second, many antismoking forces have claimed that the excise tax is the most powerful tool government possesses to affect the cigarette industry. Increases in excise tax rates, along with public smoking bans, became the favorite public policy instruments of the antismoking forces in their attempt to force the eventual demise of the cigarette industry. To ascertain the effects that excise tax increases had on the cigarette industry, two aspects of different responses to excise tax increases will be studied. First, what effect do various excise tax increases have on the sale of cigarettes? Second, can excise tax increases force cigarette firms to change their pricing policies?

3. Third, besides affecting the cigarette industry, cigarette excise taxes have a profound effect on states' finances. Again, two questions will be examined. First, do states that impose very high excise tax increases experience a Laffer (inverse) effect, that is, do revenues actually fall? Second, do neighboring states benefit from increasing sales when neighboring states impose a very high excise tax increase?

Part II

Cigarette Sales, Cigarette Prices, and State Excise Tax Policy

4

Evaluating the Effects of Second-Wave Policies on Cigarette Sales

INTRODUCTION

Since the beginning of the Second Wave (1964) and the accompanying smoking and health issue, one of the implicit aims of the federal government has been to discourage cigarette smoking. Since the coming of the Third Wave in 1986, local and state governments have become much more active in promoting antismoking measures. There have been numerous ways in which the government (at least parts of it) hopes to fulfill this goal of a "smoke-free society" (*Surgeon General*, 1985, p. 1).

In Chapter 2, it was pointed out that the traditional means that government has used to reduce cigarette consumption have been advertising bans, smoking bans, and excise taxes. Most of these governmental tools have been employed in varying intensity, and there are many current proposals to strengthen these familiar regulatory measures. Also, the effects these measures have cannot be confined strictly to cigarette consumption. Obviously, if these measures are effective in decreasing cigarette sales, then they would have an effect on the structure of the cigarette industry (particularly in regard to the number of firms that would stay committed to a dying industry) and the strategies of the cigarette firms, especially in regard to pricing policies of these firms. Hence, this current research has as its goal to examine two research questions:

1. What are the effects of the various public policy measures on U.S. cigarette sales?
2. What are the effects of these measures on the pricing strategies of the U.S. cigarette firms?

Obviously, these questions are not new. We have already pointed out previous attempts to answer them and the problems these studies have encountered, especially in the United States. The data that will be used in this present attempt to analyze these questions are unique because they involve monthly cigarette sales figures for all fifty states plus the District of Columbia from 1967 to 1986. Because the United States does not have a uniform antismoking policy (cigarette excise tax rates vary from state to state and smoking prohibition laws also differ greatly), these data give this study two advantages:

1. This state data will enable the researcher to isolate those states that have used cigarette excise tax increases as the primary tool to achieve their antismoking goals from those states that have used smoking bans as their primary weapon. There are, of course, states that have employed a combination of these measures to fulfill their goals of a smoke-free society.
2. States have also utilized these regulatory measures with varying amounts of intensity. Some states have high excise tax rates; others have low rates. The number of smoking prohibition laws also differ greatly from state to state.

To account for these differences between the various states, Figure 4.1 will divide the various states into nine different categories at the end of the Second Wave of regulation. The purpose of this chart is to isolate which particular measure a state has employed and the emphasis which that state is placing on that measure during the Second Wave of regu-lation. Because the purpose of this chapter is to analyze the effects of regulatory measures on the cigarette industry, this chart will permit the researcher to analyze cigarette sales data for a state that fulfills certain conditions. For example, if the researcher wishes to study the effect of the TV and radio cigarette advertising ban on cigarette sales in isolation, then a state should be chosen that has low cigarette excise taxes and few or no smoking prohibition laws.

This chart will be updated when we will examine the effects of excise tax increases during the Third Wave of regulation. What effect do various types of excise tax increases have on cigarette sales? Do the cigarette firms change their pricing policies when they are confronted with excise tax increases? These will be the questions presented in Chapter 5.

The primary analytical tool that will be employed is ARIMA Inter-vention analysis. The last section of this chapter will briefly summarize the results of this ARIMA Intervention analysis. The interested reader might also refer to Box and Jenkins (1976) for a thorough explanation of this technique. The chief benefit of this technique is that it allows the researcher to determine the specific shape of the impact of a public policy intervention. The reader will see how valuable this determination is as we examine various samples of cigarette sales data. However, the reader who does not wish to investigate these various statistical intricacies will not be at a disadvantage in evaluating the rest of the results of this study. This chapter will focus on the public policy measures unique to the Second Wave of regulation: the advertising ban of 1971 and the enactment by various legislatures throughout the United States of smoking bans in public places and buildings.

ADVERTISING BANS

Total advertising bans have been employed in many European countries since the early 1960s (World Health Organization, 1982, p. 59). In the United States, TV and radio cigarette advertising has been banned since 1971. Currently, there is a proposal before Congress to ban all cigarette advertising. This proposal was initially sponsored by former Congressman Synar of Oklahoma, who states as a rationale for this measure, "Finland, Norway and Sweden all experienced declines in the proportion of the population which smokes after a total advertising ban was enacted" (*Fortune*, 8/24/94, p. 74). Unfortunately, these governments also enacted other measures such as doubling the excise tax at the same time they were enacting this advertising ban, so that the cause and effect between the decline in cigarette consumption and the advertising ban is virtually impossible to verify. One of the aims of this thesis will be to isolate the effects that other measures could have had on cigarette sales when an advertising ban was imposed. Indiana is a state that fulfills these conditions.

Antismoking groups have also contended that the real effect of the advertising ban can only be measured over time. These groups contend that advertising makes cigarette smoking attractive to teenagers. So while an advertising ban would not discourage current smokers, it might decrease the number of teenagers starting the "habit" and cause cigarette sales to decline in the long run.

Figure 4.1 will be utilized to determine what the "antismoking" climate of a state was during the Second Wave of regulation. Cell (1,1) represents states with low excise taxes and few smoking prohibitions. It is not surprising to find that the six tobacco-producing states (North Carolina, South Carolina, Tennesse, Kentucky, Virginia, and Maryland) have adopted a "caveat emptor" attitude toward tobacco. Yet there are other states that also fall into this category, such as Georgia, Indiana, Missouri and Wyoming. States such as Hawaii and New York [cell (1,3)] adopted a high-tax, low-prohibitions policy toward cigarette smoking. Why Arkansas has followed this policy, though, remains a mystery.

# of Smoking Prohibition Laws	Excise Tax Rate(cents/pack)		
	Low Level (2-13/pack)	Median Level (14-20/pack)	High Level (21-31/pack)
0 - 4	GEORGIA (1,1) INDIANA KENTUCKY MARYLAND MISSOURI NORTH CAROLINA SOUTH CAROLINA TENNESSEE VIRGINIA WYOMING	ALABAMA (1,2) DELAWARE ILLINOIS LOUISIANA MISSISSIPPI NEW MEXICO OKLAHOMA PENNSYLVANIA VERMONT WEST VIRGINIA	ARKANSAS (1,3) HAWAII NEW YORK
5 - 9	(2,1) CALIFORNIA	ARIZONA (2,2) COLORADO NEVADA OHIO TEXAS	IOWA (2,3) KANSAS MAINE MASSACHUSETTS SOUTH DAKOTA D.C.
10 - 12	(3,1) IDAHO UTAH	ALASKA (3,2) MONTANA NEW HAMPSHIRE NORTH DAKOTA	(3,3) CONNECTICUT FLORIDA MICHIGAN MINNESOTA NEBRASKA NEW JERSEY OREGON RHODE ISLAND WASHINGTON WISCONSIN

Cell identification
(r,c)

Figure 4.1   States' policies toward smoking (as of 1/1/85). *Source:* Adapted from Tobacco Institute.

Meanwhile, cell (3,1) has states such as Idaho and Utah, which have passed many smoking prohibition laws but have low excise taxes. Finally, cell (3,3) has states that have a high excise tax and a high number of smoking prohibition laws. Nine of the ten states in this category are north of the Mason-Dixon line, but Florida, which produces some tobacco and has a well-developed tourist trade, also falls into this category. Overall, twenty-five states fall into these four "extreme" category cells: (1,1); (1,3); (3,1); and (3,3). The remaining five cells contain the other twenty-five states that have taken a somewhat "middle of the road" approach in their policies toward smoking cigarettes. The aim of this analysis is to examine the impact that the various public policy measures had on cigarette sales in various states, using what cell a particular state falls into as the basis of comparison.

1971 U.S. Ban on TV and Radio Advertising of Cigarettes

On January 1, 1971, all television and radio commercials for cigarettes were banned as a result of the Public Health Cigarette Smoking Act. The rationale for this legislation was that "television had given the tobacco companies a remarkable tool for persuading people to smoke" and therefore banning this advertising ought to aid in the government's antismoking campaign (Schmalense, p. 47). From 1940 to 1960, per-capita consumption of cigarettes in the adult population of the United States had nearly doubled. Since this period corresponds with the formative period of commercial television, a causal connection was thought to exist between mass media advertising and cigarette smoking (ibid., p. 52).

Using an econometric model and national data, Hamilton came to theconclusion that the ban actually led to an increase in the sales of cigarettes (Hamilton, 1972). He explained his conclusion by pointing out that "the ban disconnects the cigarette industry from the Fairness Doctrine, which offered the Government the most effective channel for promulgating health warnings" (ibid., p. 409). Since Hamilton was using national data, it was impossible for him to control for price increases. The price of cigarettes does vary state by state since each state does have a different excise tax rate, and these excise taxes account for nearly 30 percent of the retail price of cigarettes (Tobacco Institute, *Fairness Issue*, p. 1).

Thus we need to find states where the excise tax rate remained constant, that had no smoking restrictions enacted during the period after the imposition of the ban, and where the price of cigarettes continues to rise throughout the period after the advertising ban. Indiana is one of three states (the other two states being Maryland and Virginia) that fulfills all those conditions. From 1965 to 1977, Indiana's excise tax rate was constant at the low rate of 6 cents per pack. Recalling Figure 4.1, Indiana had not enacted and still has not enacted any antismoking prohibition laws. Finally, during the period from 1968 to 1977, the average price of a pack of cigarettes increased from 28 cents per pack to 51 cents per pack, which was slightly lower than the rate of inflation. Hence, if the advertising ban had an effect on sales, it ought to have been significant in Indiana. To test if the results of the ban would be different in a tobacco-producing state, either Maryland or Virginia could have been chosen. Virginia was selected for two reasons: the state has never enacted any smoking prohibition laws, and in 1966, it became the only state that actually lowered its excise tax rate on cigarettes, from 3 cents per pack to 2.5 cents per pack.

The following hypothesis was tested for both cases:

H_0: There was a gradual but permanent decrease in cigarette sales owing to the imposition of the TV and radio advertising ban of 1971.

Because it was maintained by proponents of the advertising ban that advertising makes cigarette smoking attractive, one would expect that the effects of the advertising ban would be felt in the long run because the cigarette firms would no longer be able to attract new smokers, whereas the effect of the ban would be minimal in the short run because established smokers wouldn't be affected by the ban.

In all of the analysis in this chapter, seven years of monthly data were examined: three years of data preceding an intervention and three years of data following the intervention. This will provide the reader with more than enough data to examine the effect of the intervention. It is also more than enough data to conduct the ARIMA Intervention analysis. The time series of cigarette sales for Indiana (1968–1974) is shown in Figure 4.2, where it appears that cigarette sales in Indiana were increasing throughout the time period examined. The ARIMA Intervention analysis, which is at the end of this chapter, shows that the imposition of the advertising ban had neither a positive nor a negative effect on cigarette sales. Hence, the imposition of the TV and radio advertising ban certainly did not decrease sales in Indiana, but neither can one make

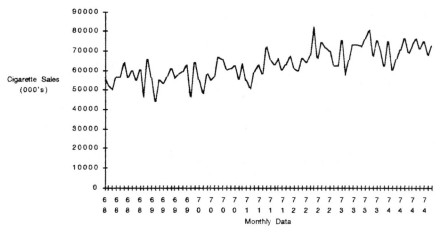

Figure 4.2 Indiana sales (1968 to 1974).

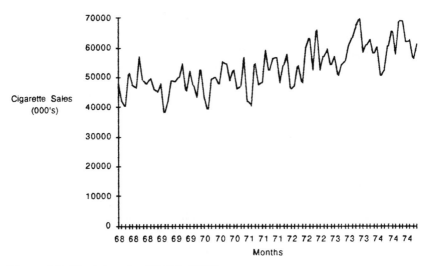

Figure 4.3 Virginia sales (1968 to 1974).

the case that the imposition of this advertising ban increased cigarette sales in Indiana.

Figure 4.3 describes cigarette sales for Virginia for the period 1968 to 1974.

Once again, there appears to be an upward trend for cigarette sales in Virginia throughout the period studied. The ARIMA results also confirm that the advertising ban had no negative or positive effect on Virginia's cigarette sales. Once again, as in the case of Indiana, the advertising ban appears to have had no effect on the sale of cigarettes.

Overall, the ARIMA Intervention analysis of sales from both Indiana and Virginia confirmed Hamilton's contention that sales did rise, although the increase was statistically insignificant. The rate of change parameter (δ) indicated that cigarette sales did rise in the long run, although this increase in sales was also statistically insignificant. Therefore, these results disclose that the advertising ban had no effect on cigarette sales either in the short or the long run.

PUBLIC SMOKING BANS

The use of public smoking bans as a measure to discourage cigarette smoking is a fairly recent phenomenon. Originally, these public smoking laws were passed to reduce the annoyance or nuisance of cigarette smoke for nonsmokers. Such restrictions typically regulate smoking in locations such as restaurants, retail stores, and sometimes the work-

place. In 1970, five states considered and rejected ten smoking restrictions laws (Tobacco Institute, *Smoking Restrictions*, 1986, p. 1).

But with the advent of the passive smoking issue, the number of
smoking restrictions bills in 1985 increased to 116 bills in thirty-seven
states; 15 of these bills were enacted in nine states (ibid., p. 2). The
argument used by proponents of this type of legislation is to emphasize
the "rights of the nonsmoker" with the hope that these measures might
also discourage the smoker from smoking (Tollison, pp. 69–70). Because
of this emphasis on the "rights of the nonsmoker," it is not surprising
that there have not been any statistical studies measuring if these laws
in any way affected cigarette sales. To measure the effectiveness of these
laws, it would be helpful if a state had passed these antismoking
restrictions while at the same time not increasing its excise tax rate. If
these conditions are fulfilled, then we ought to be able to measure the
effects that smoking prohibition laws have by themselves. Public smoking legislation varies considerably in scope; for example, a bill may be
comprehensive, regulating smoking in places of employment and
places open to the public, or it might be piecemeal, restricting smoking
in one specific place such as a retail store or a restaurant.

In 1976, Utah passed the most stringent antismoking prohibitions
enacted by any state at that time. It was illegal to smoke in the workplace (public and private), restaurants, retail stores, public transportation (including airlines), any building using state funds, and cultural
and health facilities. After this law was passed, essentially the only legal
area to smoke cigarettes in in Utah was in your own home. It certainly
seems that Utah was the one state that had anticipated the emergence
of the Third Wave of regulation. Obviously, this action by Utah was
prophetic. Utah's excise tax rate remained constant at the low level of
8 cents per pack from 1963 to 1980. If a researcher wanted to see the
effects of very stringent antismoking prohibitions, Utah's cigarette sales
should provide an ideal test case. As was the case with advertising bans,
some antismoking forces contend that the effectiveness of these laws
can only be measured in the long run.

The hypothesis that was tested assumed that these smoking prohibitions would have the same type of effect on sales as the ban on
cigarette advertising had on the sale of cigarettes, that is some current
cigarette smokers would be discouraged from smoking, but the long-
run benefit would be that these smoking bans would discourage new
smokers from picking up the habit. And so the following hypothesis
was tested:

H_0: There was a gradual but permanent decrease in cigarette sales owing
to Utah's imposition of various public smoking bans in 1976.

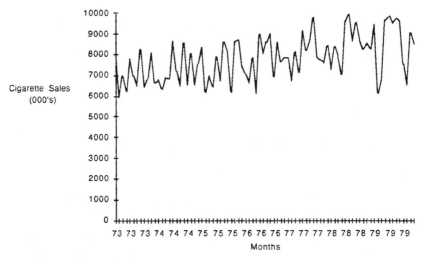

Figure 4.4 Utah sales (1973 to 1979).

The time series for Utah's cigarettes sales from 1973 to 1979 is shown in Figure 4.4. The long-term trend appears to be a steady if unspectacular increase in cigarette sales throughout the period in question. It does not appear that the passage of the smoking ban had any negative effects on Utah's cigarette sales. The ARIMA analysis shows that although sales did fall after the imposition of smoking bans this decline was not statistically significant. It also shows that the trend for cigarette sales was upward, although again this result was statistically insignificant. Overall, the imposition of the restrictions of smoking areas prove to have had no effect on cigarette sales either in the short or the long run.

Table 4.1 provides a summary of the results of this chapter. Neither the ban on all radio and TV advertising nor the enactment of strict

Table 4.1 The effects of Second-Wave public policy measures on cigarette sales.

Measure	Hypothesis	Result
Advertising Ban	(1): There was a gradual but permanent decrease in cigarette sales due to the imposition of the TV and radio cigarette advertising ban of 1971	REJECTED
Public Smoking Ban	(2): There was a gradual but permanent decrease in cigarette sales due to the imposition of of a stringent public smoking ban.	REJECTED

antismoking bans decreased the sale of cigarettes. Perhaps these measures might have been more effective if the antismoking culture would have been more developed. One could also argue that they set the stage for developing the much more stringent anti-smoking atmosphere of the Third Wave of cigarette regulation.

ARIMA RESULTS

The Federal Advertising Ban of 1971

Indiana. The time series of cigarette sales for Indiana in the period 1968–1974 (see Figure 4.2) was identified as an ARIMA model $(0,1,1)$ $(0,1,0)_{12}$. Regular and seasonal differencing achieved stationarity in the series. The MA parameters were estimated and statistically tested with the following results: $\theta_1 = .0632$ (t = 14.74); Q = 11.9 (p < .01) with 47 degrees of freedom. It is not statistically significant, that is the residuals of the model are not statistically different from white noise. So, the tentative model was accepted. The dynamic model postulated was

$$y_t = \{\omega \ B/(1 - \delta \ B)\} \ S_t^{(T)}$$

where ω and δ are the rate of change and the level of change parameter, respectively. y_t is the filtered series, B is the back space operator used to achieve a stationary mean and variance, and $S_t^{(T)}$ is the binary variable that introduces the intervention into the series. This model is consistent with the hypothesis of an expectation of a gradual decrease in cigarette sales due to the imposition of the advertising ban. The parameters estimates are $\delta = .41$ (t = .49) and $\omega = 1879.4$ (t = .04). Hence, the imposition of the TV and radio advertising ban had no effects on cigarette sales in Indiana either in the short or the long run.

Virginia. The time series of cigarette sales that describes cigarette sales for Virginia in the period 1968–1974 (see Figure 4.3) was also identified as a $(0,1,1)(0,1,0)_{12}$ ARIMA model where regular and seasonal differencing was needed to achieve stationarity in the series. The MA parameters were estimated and found statistically significant at the .01 level of significance [$\theta_1 = .0864$ (t = 11.01)]. Q = 13.4 with 47 degrees of freedom and so the residuals were found not to be statistically different from white noise. Hence, the tentative model was accepted.

The dynamic model postulated was the same one used to test the Indiana data. The parameter estimates were: $\delta = .11$ (t = .22) and $\omega = 1,851.6$ (t = .24). The results again show that the advertising ban had no negative effect on cigarette sales.

Smoking Prohibition Laws

The time series for Utah's cigarettes sales in the period 1973–1979 is shown in Figure 4.4. The series includes three years of monthly figures before the intervention and four years of monthly figures after the intervention in 1976. The ARIMA model for this series was identified as a $(1,1,1)(0,1,1)_{12}$. Regular and seasonal differencing were needed to achieve stationarity in this series. The AR parameter was estimated with the following result: $o = -.5040$ ($t = -2.90$). The MA parameters were found to be: $\theta_1 = .5909$ ($t = 5.62$) and $\theta_{12} = .4404$ ($t = 2.63$). Since the Q statistic was 16.4 with 24 degrees of freedom ($p < .01$), the null hypothesis that the residuals were "white noise" was not rejected. Hence, the model was accepted.

The dynamic model postulated was $y_t = \{\omega\ B\ /\ (1 - \delta B)\ \}\ S_t^{(T)}$ where ω and δ are the level of change and the rate of change parameters respectively. The model is consistent with the hypothesis of an expectation of a gradual decrease in cigarette sales due to the imposition of the smoking bans. The parameter values estimated were $\delta = .0538$ ($t = .10$) and $\omega = -207$ ($t = -.72$). These results indicate that the null hypothesis of a gradual decrease in sales due to the imposition of the smoking bans ought to be rejected. The analysis shows that although sales did fall after the imposition of smoking bans this decline was not statistically significant. It also shows that the trend for cigarette sales was upward although again this result was statistically insignificant. Overall, the imposition of the restrictions of smoking areas proves to have no effect on cigarette sales either in the short or the long run.

The Cigarette Excise Tax: The Public Policy Measure of the Third Wave of Regulation

INTRODUCTION

In the previous chapter, we concluded that the unique public policy measures of the Second Wave of regulation (advertising bans, smoking bans) had no measurable effect on cigarettes sales. However, although the antismoking policies were ineffective, the overall trend of cigarette sales was certainly declining by .5 percent per year. The connection between smoking and illness had been established and smokers were trying to quit.

As was pointed out in Chapter 2, the Third Wave of regulation was stimulated by the passive smoking issue and resulted in a marked increase in the number of public policy initiatives to regulate where an individual can smoke and to discourage cigarette smoking. There are twelve types of cigarette smoking restrictions that have been proposed: (1) Any public building posted as "No Smoking"; (2) elevators; (3) public transportation; (4) educational facilities; (5) cultural facilities; (6) health care facilities; (7) government-owned building/public meetings; (8) food stores; (9) retail stores; (10) restaurants; (11) workplace-government; (12) workplace-private sector. Although none of these restrictions are new, the number of states and local governments that became interested in enacting them increased dramatically as was illustrated previously in Figure 2.2 (p. 37).

This burst of legislative activity was not just confined to the state and local levels of government. Figure 2.3 (p. 37) also illustrated that congressional interest in the smoking issue has increased dramatically since 1987. There have been numerous proposals to restrict smoking in federal buildings and to discourage smoking in the military.

But while the majority of these legislative proposals at the federal, state, and local levels of government were concerned with smoking restrictions, the public policy measure that became the focal point of conflict between the cigarette industry and its zealous critics was the excise tax. If we examine Figure 5.1, we can readily see the important role the excise tax has played not only in discouraging cigarette use but in reshaping the cigarette industry itself.

The reader should refer to Figure 4.1 (p. 68) so that a comparison can be made between it and Figure 5.1. In making this comparison, differences between the Second and the Third Waves of regulation will become quite obvious. First, we will concentrate on the number of smoking prohibition laws during each wave. In Figure 4.1, we see that nearly half (46 percent) the states had only between 0 and 4 smoking prohibition laws during the Second Wave of regulation whereas 31 percent of the states had between 10 and 12 smoking prohibition laws. However, when we examine Figure 5.1, we notice that during the Third Wave of regulation, there is a complete reversal of the pattern established during the Second Wave of regulation with 46 percent of the states having between 10 and 12 smoking prohibition laws and only 26 percent having between 0 and 4 smoking prohibition laws. There has certainly been a substantial increase in the use of smoking prohibitions as part of the Third Wave of regulation of the cigarette industry. However, as we saw in the previous chapter, these laws appear to have little or no effect on cigarette sales. Therefore, although these measures are largely symbolic, they allow public policy makers to signal antismoking forces that their legislative agenda will be taken seriously.

The other significant change that has occurred during the Third Wave of regulation has been the dramatic increase in the level of excise tax rates on cigarettes. At the end of the Second Wave of regulation, excise tax rates ranged from 2 cents per pack to 31 cents per pack. During the ten years of the Third Wave of regulation, the range of cigarette excise tax rates has more than doubled from 2.5 cents per pack to 65 cents per pack. The average state excise tax has also nearly doubled from 16 cents per pack at the end of the Second Wave of regulation to 30 cents per pack at the end of 1994. At the same time, there have been proposals to increase the federal excise tax rate from 32 cents per pack to 75 cents per pack (Tobacco Institute, *The Tax Burden on Tobacco*, 1994, p. 1).

Proponents of cigarette excise tax rate increases have given three rationales to justify these dramatic increases: (1) to discourage the use of cigarettes; (2) to influence the pricing policies of cigarette firms ; and (3) to provide revenue for governmental programs.

The remaining parts of this chapter will examine the first two points, the power of the cigarette excise tax to decrease cigarette sales and to

# of Smoking Prohibition Laws	Excise Tax Rate(cents/pack)		
	Low Level (2.5-20/pack)	Median Level (21-40/pack)	High Level (41-65/pack)
0 - 4	ALABAMA (1,1) GEORGIA INDIANA KENTUCKY MISSISSIPPI NORTH CAROLINA TENNESSEE WEST VIRGINIA WYOMING	ARKANSAS (1,2) DELAWARE NEW MEXICO	TEXAS (1,3)
5 - 9	ARIZONA (2,1) COLORADO IDAHO SOUTH CAROLINA	CALIFORNIA (2,2) MARYLAND MICHIGAN OHIO OKLAHOMA SOUTH DAKOTA	CONNECTICUT (2,3) D.C. MASSACHUSETTS NORTH DAKOTA
10 - 12	(3,1) LOUISIANA MISSOURI MONTANA VERMONT VIRGINIA	ALASKA FLORIDA IOWA (3,2) KANSAS MAINE NEBRASKA NEVADA NEW HAMPSHIRE NEW JERSEY OREGON PENNSYLVANIA UTAH WISCONSIN	(3,3) HAWAII ILLINOIS NEW YORK RHODE ISLAND WASHINGTON

Cell identification
(r,c)

Figure 5.1 States' policies toward smoking (as of 7/1/94).

change the pricing polices of the cigarette firms. The third point will be dealt with as a separate issue in Chapter 6.

THE EFFECT OF CIGARETTE EXCISE TAX INCREASES ON CIGARETTE SALES

The measure that government at all levels has employed most frequently to discourage the sale of cigarettes is the cigarette excise tax. In

Chapter 2, it was pointed out that this tax was first employed by the federal government in 1865 to raise funds to pay for the Civil War but it had the unintended consequence of reducing tobacco consumption (Tennant, p. 131). In 1921, Iowa became the first state to impose an excise tax on cigarettes (ibid., p. 133). By 1983, every state had imposed this tax, with North Carolina being the last state to enact a cigarette excise tax. The primary purpose of the excise tax until the 1980s was to raise revenue. In the 1980s, starting with the doubling of the federal excise tax in 1983, the cigarette excise tax started being used as a weapon to discourage cigarette smoking.

In this chapter, we will examine the effects of various state excise tax increases during the Third Wave of regulation. Three types of increases will be investigated:

1. A small excise tax increase—less than 10 cents per pack
2. A moderate excise tax increase—between 10 cents per pack and 15 cents per pack
3. A large excise tax increase—greater than 15 cents per pack.

Along with examining each type of excise tax increase, the various levels of smoking prohibition laws will also be taken into consideration. Six cases will be analyzed and will be fitted to one of the following ARIMA Intervention models.

First Hypothesis:

H_0: With the imposition of an excise tax increase, there was an abrupt and permanent decrease in cigarette sales.

This model is the equivalent of a step function in an econometric model. If this model fails, then a second model will be tested that will have the following hypothesis:

Second Hypothesis:

H_0: With the imposition of an excise tax increase, there was a slow but permanent decline in cigarette sales.

This model assumes that the excise tax increase will add impetus to the decline in cigarette sales.

Third Hypothesis:

H_0: With the imposition of an excise tax increase, there was an immediate decrease in cigarette sales followed by a gradual return to pre-intervention levels.

It should be pointed out that one of the advantages of ARIMA modeling is that it allows the researcher to model exactly what the change in the series resembled and hence, will permit the policy maker to make judgments on the effectiveness of these various public policy measures.

Small Excise Tax Increase (Less than 10 Cents per Pack)

Even though the antismoking forces have become much stronger with the coming of the Third Wave of regulation, the vast majority of state excise tax increases during this period were still less than 10 cents per pack. These small cigarette excise tax increases were enacted to placate antismoking forces and to balance a state's budget. In this section, we will examine the effect of these small excise tax increases on the sale of cigarettes in two different cases, one state with very few smoking prohibition laws, and another state with many more smoking prohibition laws. Figure 5.1 will be used in selecting these states.

Wyoming. Wyoming's attitude toward the smoking and health issue has been largely one of "laissez-faire." It has a low excise tax rate (the excise tax was last increased from 8 cents per pack to 12 cents per pack on 1/1/90) and still has not enacted any smoking prohibition laws. Wyoming is a western state with a small, rural population that separates it from the other states in the category of low excise tax rate and few smoking prohibition laws.

The time series of cigarette sales for Wyoming is shown in Figure 5.2. Again, for the interested reader, the ARIMA Intervention analysis can be found in the appendix of this chapter.

The imposition of a small excise tax increase in 1990 appears to have had no effect on the slightly downward turn that cigarette sales in Wyoming experienced throughout the period from 1987 to 1993. The ARIMA Intervention analysis confirms this observation. Thus, the sale of cigarettes in Wyoming appears to have been unaffected by a small excise tax increase. Yet the indifference shown by public policy toward the smoking and health issue has also not been able to slow the gradual decline in cigarette sales.

Louisiana. In August 1990, Louisiana's cigarette excise tax rate increased from 16 cents per pack to 20 cents per pack. Louisiana has also passed all of the smoking prohibition laws except for banning smoking in any public building. Although this increase in the cigarette excise tax is small, it does occur in a state that had been fairly active in promoting an antismoking environment.

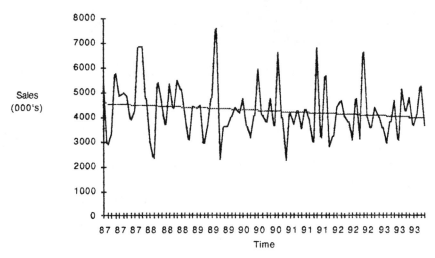

Figure 5.2 Wyoming sales (1987 to 1993). *Source:* Adapted from Tobacco Institute.

Figure 5.3 shows the time series representation of cigarette sales for Louisiana from 1987 to 1993. Throughout the period analyzed, Louisiana's cigarette sales were declining. But, as was the case with Wyoming, the imposition of a small cigarette excise does not appear to have hastened the decline of cigarette sales. The ARIMA Intervention

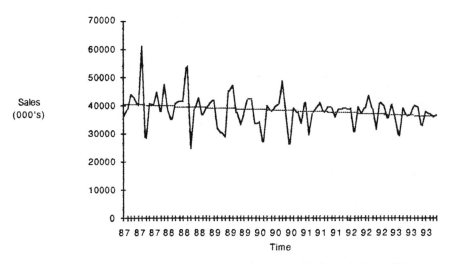

Figure 5.3 Louisiana sales (1987 to 1993). *Source:* Adapted from Tobacco Institute.

analysis also confirms this assertion. Even though the antismoking culture appears to be stronger in Louisiana than in Wyoming, the effect of a small excise tax increase appears to be the same: there was no statistically significant difference in the rate of decline of cigarette sales. Overall, the imposition of a small excise tax appears to have one effect; it brings additional revenue to a state government while leaving cigarette sales unaffected.

Moderate Excise Tax Increases (Between 10 Cents per Pack and 15 Cents per Pack)

With the coming of the Third Wave of regulation, there was much greater pressure on state legislatures to enact cigarette excise tax increases of greater magnitude than occurred during the Second Wave of regulation. The one obvious reason was the need for revenue. Others contended that cigarette smokers should pay for the additional health services they require because of cigarette smoking. Finally, antismoking forces contend that higher cigarette excise taxes will discourage cigarette smoking, especially in the young, by making cigarettes too expensive for them. The same criteria that was used for selecting states in the previous section will be used for these moderate excise tax increases.

Texas. On June 1, 1990, Texas increased its cigarette excise tax from 26 cents per pack to 41 cents per pack. With that increase, Texas had the highest cigarette excise tax in the nation. But while the Texas legislature was quite content to tax Texan smokers at the highest rate in the country, it did not restrict the smoking habits of Texan smokers. There were only four public areas where smokers were restricted: elevators, educational facilities, health care facilities, and public transportation.

Figure 5.4 shows the time series for Texas cigarette sales from 1987 to 1993. Texas cigarette sales were declining throughout the period analyzed. With the imposition of this cigarette excise tax increase, there was a significant drop in cigarette sales. But the ARIMA Intervention analysis corresponds to the Third Hypothesis, listed earlier in this chapter. It shows that sales declined at a much greater rate than had occurred before the imposition of the excise tax increase but cigarette sales gradually returned to their previous rate of decline. It appears that Texas cigarette smokers rebelled at first at the increase in excise taxes but eventually accepted the higher prices caused by the excise tax increase.

Rhode Island. Rhode Island has consistently implemented a very stringent antismoking policy. In both the Second and Third Waves of regulation, Rhode Island has been in cell (3,3). It is a state that has high excise

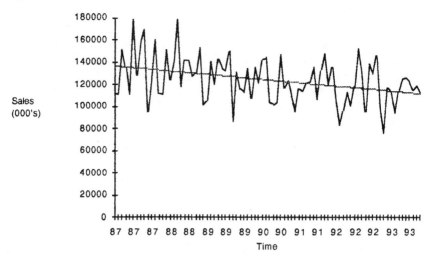

Figure 5.4   Texas sales (1987 to 1993). *Source:* Adapted from Tobacco Institute.

tax rates and at least ten smoking prohibition laws. In August 1989, Rhode Island raised its cigarette excise tax from 27 cents per pack to 37 cents per pack. With this increase, Rhode Island appeared to be trying to strengthen its already rather strong antismoking policies.

Rhode Island's cigarette sales for the period 1987 to 1993 are displayed in Figure 5.5. The ARIMA Intervention model that best fits Rhode Island's sales is one in which there has been a slow but steady decline of cigarette sales. In other words, although this excise tax increase did not lead to a dramatic decrease in cigarette sales, it did lead to a speedup in the rate of decrease.

It should be noted that the 1989 cigarette excise tax rate increase was the second of three increases in the cigarette excise rate that Rhode Island has instituted since the inception of the Third Wave. There was a 2 cents per pack increase in 1987 and another 7 cents per pack increase in 1993. Hence, it appears that Rhode Island's strategy of a series of small and moderate increases in its cigarette excise tax, along with its passage of antismoking laws, has been successful in decreasing cigarette sales at a pace greater than the national average.

Large Excise Tax Increase (Greater than 15 Cents per Pack)

As the Third Wave of regulation gathered momentum, the potential of enacting very large cigarette excise tax increases became a distinct

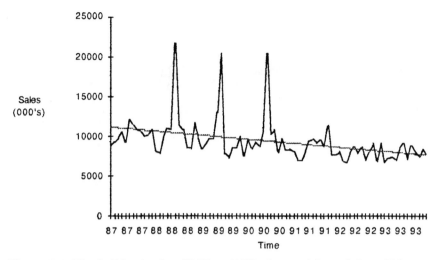

Figure 5.5 Rhode Island sales (1987 to 1993). *Source:* Adapted from Tobacco Institute.

possibility. Antismoking activists were convinced that the cigarette excise tax was the most potent weapon in the hands of public policy makers. However, no longer would a small excise tax increase satisfy these antismoking forces, who fully realized that only large cigarette excise tax increases could accomplish their goal of a smoke-free society. Once again, we will examine the effects of two large cigarette excise tax increases in states that have different numbers of smoking prohibition laws.

Massachusetts. In contrast to Rhode Island's policy of instituting a series of small and moderate cigarette excise tax increases, Massachusetts's response to the Third Wave of regulation was to dramatically raise its cigarette excise tax rate from 26 cents per pack to 51 cents per pack. This increase was instituted on January 1, 1993. But although the Massachusetts state legislature was willing to raise the cigarette excise tax, it only enacted seven out of a possible twelve smoking prohibition laws. Thus, it appears that Massachusetts was using the excise as the primary weapon in its antismoking policy.

Figure 5.6 shows the time series for Massachusetts's cigarette sales from 1988 to 1994. This graph shows that there was an immediate decline in cigarette sales. The ARIMA Intervention analysis that fitted the Massachusetts cigarette sales data corresponds to the hypothesis

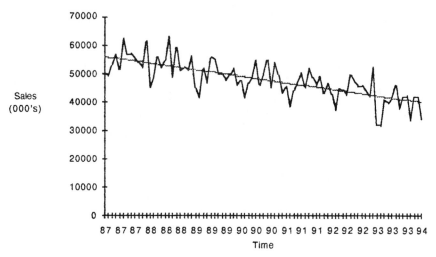

Figure 5.6 Massachusetts sales (1987 to 1993). *Source:* Adapted from Tobacco Institute.

that there was an immediate and permanent decline in cigarette sales. Therefore, the ARIMA analysis not only confirms the decline in sales but shows that this decline was permanent.

Washington. The state of Washington has traditionally been a leader in developing an effective antismoking policy. Every smoking prohibition law has been passed, and it entered the Third Wave of regulation with one of the highest cigarette tax rates at 31 cents per pack, which was raised to 34 cents per pack in 1990. Then, in July 1993, Washington raised its cigarette excise tax rate again to 54 cents per pack.

The time series that describes Washington's cigarette sales from 1987 to 1994 is shown in Figure 5.7. As was the case with Massachusetts, the effect of this large cigarette excise tax increase was that there was a sharp and permanent decline in cigarette sales; the ARIMA Intervention analysis confirmed this observation.

Overall, the cigarette excise tax has proven to be the most effective public policy measure in decreasing cigarette sales if public policy makers have the will to raise the rate substantially. In the case of Rhode Island, we have seen how even a series of small and moderate cigarette excise tax rate hikes can lead to an above average decrease in cigarette sales. We have also seen that the momentum of the Third Wave of regulation has led to some very large cigarette tax increases on both the state and federal levels of government.

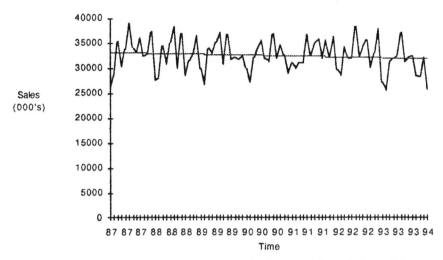

Figure 5.7 Washington sales (1987 to 1994). *Source:* Adapted from Tobacco Institute.

Antismoking groups have another hope for cigarette excise tax increases, namely, that these increases ought to reduce the profits that cigarette firms earn on their cigarette sales not only by cutting into cigarette sales but also by forcing the cigarette firms to hold back on price increases. To find out whether cigarette firms are indeed sensitive to these excise tax increases will be the objective of the final section of this chapter.

CIGARETTE EXCISE TAXES AND THE PRICING POLICIES OF CIGARETTE FIRMS

With the arrival of the Third Wave of regulation, we have seen that an ideology of antismoking has developed that is much more aggressive in eliminating not only cigarette smoking but the firms that produce cigarettes. Because of this new ideology, there has been renewed interest in analyzing why the cigarette industry is such an incredibly profitable one. The one area in which economists have concentrated their efforts in trying to answer that question concerns the relationship between cigarette excise taxes and the pricing policies of the cigarette firms.

Because excise taxes form such a high percentage of the retail price of cigarettes (30 percent of the average nationwide retail price according to the Tobacco Institute) economists hope to use the excise tax increases as an indicator of an oligopolistic behavior on the part of the cigarette industry. If the cigarette industry was behaving in an oligopolistic manner in the face of an excise tax increase, then the industry would raise prices despite the increase in the excise tax rate.

Jeffrey Harris, an MIT economist who happens also to be a medical doctor, has been one of the most vocal critics of the cigarette industry. Harris has repeatedly charged that "cigarettes are sold in this country by a six-company oligopoly that has demonstrated the market power to raise prices at will" (Harris, *New York Times*, 1/30/87, p. 57). Harris bases his contention that the industry uses excise tax increases as an excuse for "pushing up the retail price of cigarettes far beyond the levels justified by the excise tax hike" (*Business Week*, 2/9/94, p. 21). Harris has pointed out that price hikes have far outpaced increases in excise tax rates even during this Third Wave of regulation.

Harris's contention that cigarette firms are using excise tax increases as an excuse for "unjustified" price hikes is one that needs to be examined. As I have noted earlier, the cigarette excise tax rate varies greatly from to state. As a result of these differences in excise tax rates, it would be interesting to investigate whether the cigarette firms have developed different pricing strategies to deal with these different levels of taxation.

To test whether the cigarette firms did exhibit an oligopolistic manner, as Harris has charged, when they encountered a cigarette excise tax increase at the state level, we will examine three cases:

H_0: The percentage of the retail price for cigarettes that excise taxes account for will significantly increase when a small excise tax increase is imposed.

H_0: The percentage of the retail price for cigarettes that excise taxes account for will significantly increase when a moderate excise tax increase is imposed.

H_0: The percentage of the retail price for cigarettes that excise taxes account for will significantly increase when a large excise tax increase is imposed.

Wisconsin. Wisconsin's antismoking policy has relied on a combination of smoking prohibition laws (eleven out of a possible twelve laws) and a moderately high cigarette excise rate. In May 1992, Wisconsin raised its cigarette excise tax by 8 cents per pack, thereby making its cigarette excise tax rate 38 cents per pack, which was about 10 cents above the mean state cigarette excise tax.

If we examine Figure 5.8, it appears that this small excise tax increase had no significant effect on the pricing strategies of cigarette firms in Wisconsin. The ARIMA Intervention analysis confirms this observa-

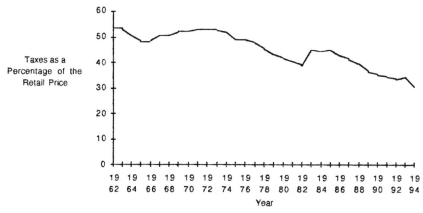

Figure 5.8 Wisconsin sales (1962 to 1994). *Source:* Adapted from Tobacco Institute.

tion. Although there was a slight rise in the percentage of the retail price accounted for by cigarette excise taxes, this rise was statistically insignificant. Hence, it appears that a small cigarette excise tax increase had little or no effect on the pricing policies of cigarette firms.

Arkansas. Arkansas's antismoking policy is typical of Southwestern States: few if any smoking prohibitions but moderate or even high cigarette excise tax rates. In February 1993, Arkansas raised its cigarette excise tax rate from 22 cents per pack to 34.5 cents per pack, a 12.5 cent increase per pack. Because most of its neighboring states had either raised or were in the process of raising their cigarette excise tax rates, Arkansas was merely joining in a movement to raise cigarette excise taxes.

Figure 5.9 shows the time series that represents the percentage of the retail price of cigarettes that can be associated with cigarette excise taxes. The graph shows that the cigarette firms did appear to hold down price increases for 1993, since the cigarette excise tax appears to be a higher percentage of the retail price for cigarettes. The ARIMA Intervention analysis points out that this rise was barely significant and that this percentage proceeded to go down immediately the next year. Thus, it does appear that this moderate rise did temporarily slow down price hikes on the part of cigarette firms, but its effect on the pricing policies of the cigarette firms was short-lived at best.

District of Columbia. D.C. has relied on the cigarette excise as the cornerstone of its antismoking policy. In July 1993, D.C. raised its

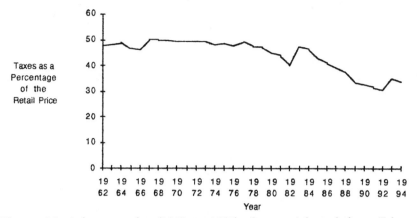

Figure 5.9 Arkansas sales (1962 to 1994). *Source:* Adapted from Tobacco Institute.

cigarette excise tax from 50 cents per pack to 65 cents per pack, the highest cigarette excise tax rate in the nation. Hence, D.C.'s cigarette excise tax policy ought to have a significant impact on the pricing policy of cigarette firms.

Figure 5.10 clearly shows that this large cigarette excise tax increase had a major impact on any planned price increases by cigarette firms. The ARIMA Intervention analysis confirms that this large cigarette excise tax increase had an impact of much greater duration than the one for the moderate cigarette excise tax increase. Thus, it appears that cigarette firms are quite sensitive to large cigarette excise tax increases.

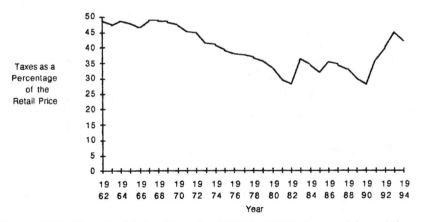

Figure 5.10 District of Columbia sales (1962 to 1994). *Source:* Adapted from Tobacco Institute.

Overall, it appears that only large increases in cigarette excise tax rates can influence the pricing policies of cigarette firms. Harris's assertion that cigarette firms use cigarette excise tax increases as an excuse to make "unjustified" price increases is correct when the excise tax increase is either small or moderate, whereas large cigarette tax increases seem to be able to hold down planned price hikes.

CONCLUSION

In the previous chapter, we saw how the policy instruments of the Second Wave regulation, that is, advertising bans and smoking prohibition laws, were ineffectual in affecting cigarette sales. In this chapter, we have witnessed how the cigarette excise tax has been used throughout the Third Wave of regulation as a means to hasten the decline in cigarette sales. There were two strategic uses of the cigarette excise tax, both of which led to a decline in cigarette sales: (1) public policy makers could institute a series of small and moderate cigarette excise tax increases in which the increases are implemented every two years; Rhode Island used this strategy to speed up the decline of cigarette sales. (2) Another strategy that has successfully reduced cigarette sales has involved a large hike in the cigarette excise tax rates (of at least 15 cents per pack). Both Massachusetts and Washington have employed this strategy. It certainly appears that this more intensive use of the cigarette excise tax has proven to be an effective measure in decreasing cigarette sales.

But besides decreasing cigarette sales, these large increases in the cigarette excise tax also appear to be effective in influencing the pricing policies of cigarette firms. The District of Columbia's cigarette excise tax policy has certainly forced the cigarette firms from making big price hikes at the retail level. As one would expect, the impact on pricing policies of cigarette firms is directly correlated with the intensity of the cigarette excise tax increase, that is, if the cigarette excise tax hike is small, its impact on cigarette-pricing policy is small.

In the next chapter, we will examine the other goal of the cigarette excise tax—to raise funds for government. Before the Third Wave of regulation, this was the one and only purpose of the cigarette excise tax. Two aspects will be examined: (1) Have any states increased their cigarette excise tax rates to such an extent that cigarette excise tax revenues have actually fallen as a result of these excise tax increases? (2) Do states compete with one another in setting their cigarette excise tax rates?

ARIMA INTERVENTION ANALYSIS

Cigarette Excise Tax Hikes and Cigarette Sales

Wyoming. The time series of cigarette sales for Wyoming (Figure 5.2) was identified as an ARIMA $(0,1,1)$ $(0,1,0)_{12}$. Again, regular and seasonal differencing achieved stationarity in the series. The MA parameter was estimated and statistically tested with the following results: θ_1 = .6021 (t =11.11) and Q = 18 with 36 degrees of freedom (p<.01). We cannot reject that the residuals form white noise and hence, the model is accepted. The first dynamic model postulated was

$$y_t = \omega \, B \, S_t^{(T)}$$

where ω is the level of change parameter. This model is consistent with a hypothesis of an expectation of a sudden and permanent decrease in sales. The parameter value was ω = −288.9 (t = −.58). There was a decrease in sales but it was determined that it was not statistically significant. The second dynamic model postulated was:

$$y_t = \{\omega B/(1 - \delta B)\} S_t^{(T)}$$

where ω is the rate change with δ = .1, implying the change is abrupt, and δ = .9, implying that the change is quite gradual; ω is the level of change parameters; y_t is the filtered series; B is the backshift operator used to achieve a stationary mean and variance; and $S_t^{(T)}$ is the binary variable that introduces the "step" intervention into the series. With this model, it was hypothesized that sales went down gradually after the imposition of the excise tax. The parameter values estimated were

$$\delta = .1619 \; (t = -.38) \text{ and } \omega = -308 \; (t = -.65).$$

These statistics indicate that although the level of sales dropped as a result of the excise tax increase, it was not statistically significant. Sales in the long run were still declining at the same rate that they were before the imposition of this excise tax increase. Therefore, these results indicate that the small rise in the cigarette excise rate had little or no effect on cigarette sales in Wyoming.

Louisiana. The time series for Louisiana's cigarette sales (Figure 5. 3) was identified as an ARIMA $(0,1,1)$ $(0,1,0)_{12}$. The MA parameter was estimated and was found statistically significant at the .01 level of confidence with the following results: θ_1 = .7416 (t = 9.19); Q = 17.8 with 36 degrees of freedom (p < .01), and hence, the model was accepted.

The first dynamic model postulated was

$$y_t = \omega \, B \, S_t^{(T)}$$

where ω is the level of change parameter. Again, this model is consistent with a hypothesis of an expectation of a sudden and permanent decrease in sales. The parameters value was

$$\omega = -580.2 \ (t = -.64).$$

Once again, there was a decrease in sales but it proved to be statistically insignificant.

The second dynamic model postulated was:

$$y_t = \{ \omega \, B / (1 - B) \} \, S_t^{(T)}.$$

This model is consistent with the hypothesis that sales went down gradually after the excise tax increase. The parameter values were estimated as

$$\delta = -.17 \ (t = -.51) \text{ and } \omega = -705.6 \ (t = -.62).$$

These results, like those of Wyoming, show that although sales did continue to fall after the excise tax increase, the rate of change of sales did not change, nor was there a one-time significant fall in cigarette sales after the cigarette excise tax rise. Once again, the small cigarette excise tax increase seemed to have no effect on cigarette sales.

Texas. The time series of cigarettes sales from 1987 to 1993 for Texas (see Figure 5.4) was identified as an ARIMA $(1,1,1) \, (0,1,1)_{12}$. The parameters were estimated and found to be statistically significant ($p<.05$).

$$\varphi_1 = -.5329 \ (t = -2.88) \quad \theta_1 = -.4658 \ (t = -10.84) \quad \theta_{12} = -.7626 \ (t = -2.86)$$

$Q = 12.8$ with 36 degrees of freedom and so the model's residuals are white noise and the tentative model is accepted.

The first model postulated was:

$$y_t = \omega \, B \, S_t^{(T)}$$

The parameter value was $\omega = -6886.8 \ (t = -1.37)$. The permanent impact of the excise tax increase appears to be statistically insignificant. A model was postulated that corresponds to the Third Hypothesis:

$y_t = \{\omega B/(1+\delta)\}\ P_t^{(T)}$ with the following results:
$\omega = -9158.9\ (t = -2.59),\ \delta = .33\ (t = 2.85).$

These results indicate that cigarette sales went down initially in reaction to the excise tax increase and then sales gradually returned to their former rate of decline.

Rhode Island. Figure 5.5 (Rhode Island's cigarette sales from 1987 to 1993) was identified as an ARIMA $(1,1,0)\ (0,1,1)_{12}$. The parameters were estimated and found to be statistically significant (p<.05):

$\varphi_1 = -.6163\ (t = -3.21),\quad \theta_{12} = -.5462\ (t = -2.83)$

Q = 21.2 with 36 degrees of freedom and so the model's residuals are white noise and the tentative model is accepted.

The first model postulated was

$y_t = \omega\ B\ S_t^{(T)}$

The parameter value was: $\omega = -2381\ (t = -.80)$. The permanent impact of the excise tax increase appears to be statistically insignificant. A model was postulated that corresponds to the Third Hypothesis:

$y_t = \{\omega B/(1+\delta)\}\ P_t^{(T)}$ with the following results:
$\omega = -9158.9\ (t = -.93),\ \delta = -.28\ (t = -4.22).$

These results indicate that cigarette sales did not go down significantly at first but the rate of decrease in cigarette sales did rise.

Massachusetts. The time series of cigarette sales for Massachusetts (Figure 5.6) was identified as an ARIMA $(0,1,1)\ (0,1,1)_{12}$. Again, regular and seasonal differencing achieved stationarity in the series. The MA parameter was estimated and statistically tested with the following results: $\theta_1 = -.4821\ (t = -7.23);\ \theta_{12} = -.3529\ (t = -2.84);$ and Q = 17.3 with 36 degrees of freedom (p.<01). We cannot reject that the residuals form white noise and hence, the model is accepted.

The first dynamic model postulated was

$y_t = \omega\ B\ S_t^{(T)}$

where ω is the level of change parameter. This model is consistent with a hypothesis of an expectation of a sudden and permanent decrease in sales. The parameter value was $\omega = -9,879\ (t = -3.85)$. There was a statistically significant decrease in sales, and the drop in sales lasted the entire time period after the imposition of the cigarette excise tax increase.

Washington. The time series of cigarette sales for Washington (Figure 5.7) was identified as an ARIMA $(1,1,1)$ $(1,1,0)_{12}$. Again, regular and seasonal differencing achieved stationarity in the series. The AR and MA parameters were estimated and statistically tested with the following results: $\varphi_1 = -.3764$ (t = −2.21); $\theta_1 = -.5211$ (t = −3.02); $\varphi_{12} = -.2769$ (t = −2.56); and Q = 19.6 with 36 degrees of freedom (p<.01). We cannot reject that the residuals form white noise and thus, the model is accepted.

The first dynamic model postulated was

$$y_t = \omega \ B \ S_t^{(T)}$$

where ω is the level of change parameter. This model is consistent with a hypothesis of an expectation of a sudden and permanent decrease in sales. The parameter value was $\omega = -4,969$ (t = −2.69). As in the case of Masschusetts, there was a statistically significant decrease in sales, and the drop in sales lasted the entire time period after the imposition of the cigarette excise tax increase.

Cigarette Excise Taxes and Pricing Strategies

Wisconsin. To ascertain the effect of the 1992 cigarette excise tax increase on retail prices of cigarettes in Wisconsin, an ARIMA model $(0,1,1)$ was employed. The parameters were estimated and found to be statistically significant at the .01 level with the following results: $\theta = -.1092$ (t = −.3.52) with Q = 8.9 with 30 degrees of freedom. The tentative model was accepted because the residuals constitute white noise.

The dynamic intervention model that was postulated hypothesized that the excise tax hike resulted in an abrupt increase in the percentage of the retail price that excise taxes made up, followed by a gradual decline to preintervention levels. The following model fulfils the preceding specifications:

$$y_t = \{ \ wB/ \ (1 - \delta B)\} \ P_t^{(T)}.$$

The parameter values were found to be $\omega = 9.108$ (t = .27), = .1092 (t = .31). The dynamic model was found to be significant at the .05 level.

The results indicate that cigarette firms fail to respond to a low cigarette excise tax increase. Because the percentage of the retail price due to cigarette excise taxes failed to rise as a result of this low increase in the excise tax, cigarette firms were able to get at least their usual yearly price increase. One might make the case that they actually used the cigarette excise tax increase as an excuse to raise prices more than they would have if no excise tax increase had occurred.

Arkansas. An ARIMA model (0,1,1) was used to fit the data shown in Figure 5.9. The parameters were estimated and found to be statistically significant at the .05 level with the following results: θ = −.4580 (t = −3.52), because Q = 11.5 with 30 degrees of freedom. The tentative model was accepted because the residuals constitute white noise.

The dynamic intervention model that was postulated hypothesized that the excise tax hike resulted in an abrupt increase in the percentage of the retail price that excise taxes made up, followed by a gradual decline to preintervention levels. The following model fulfils the preceding specifications:

$$y_t = \{\, wB/\,(1 - \delta B)\}\, P_t^{(T)}$$

The parameter values were found to be: ω = 3.74 (t = 1.97), = −.08 (t =−2.31). The dynamic model was found to be significant at the .05 level.

The results indicate that cigarette firms did respond to this moderate cigarette excise tax increase. The percentage of the retail price due to cigarette excise taxes did rise as a result of this low increase in the excise tax. However, the cigarette firms were able to raise prices in the period after the moderate cigarette excise tax increase. Therefore, although this moderate excise tax increase deterred the cigarette firms from making their usual yearly price increase, it had no effect on the long-term pricing policy of cigarette firms.

District of Columbia. Once again, an ARIMA model (0,1,1) was employed to describe the relationship between the price of cigarettes and the cigarette excise tax for D.C. (Figure 5.10). The parameters were estimated and found to be statistically significant at the .01 level with the following results: φ = .7252 (t = −2.45) with Q = 18.6 with 30 degrees of freedom. The tentative model was accepted because the residuals constitute white noise.

The dynamic intervention model which was postulated was one which hypotheisized that the excise tax hike resulted in an abrupt increase in the percentage of the retail price which excise taxes made up, followed by a gradual decline to preintervention levels. The following model fulfils the above specifications:

$$y_t = \{ wB/ (1 - \delta B)\} \, P_t^{(T)}$$

The parameter values were found to be: $\omega = 10.6$ ($t = 3.27$), $\delta = -.1092$ ($t = -.31$). The dynamic model was found to be significant at the .05 level.

The results indicate that cigarette firms did respond to a large cigarette excise tax increase. Because the percentage of the retail price due to cigarette excise taxes failed to rise as a result of this low increase in the excise tax, cigarette firms were able to get at least their usual yearly price increase. Even more striking is the result that the cigarette firms seem to refrain from raising cigarette prices in the period after this large increase in excise taxes. It certainly appears that large cigarette tax increases are quite capable of influencing the pricing policies of cigarette firms for a substantial period of time.

The States and Cigarette Excise Taxes: Dependency, Revenue, and Competition

INTRODUCTION

One of the lasting impacts of the Reagan revolution has been the shifting of responsibility for social programs from the federal to the state level of government. State governments have been forced to expand existing sources of revenue or sponsor new ones.

One source of revenue that state officials had traditionally used to balance their budgets is the "sin" tax (i.e., the excise tax on alcohol and cigarettes) in addition to taxes on gasoline, telephone calls, heating and electricity, and car registrations. But, ironically, just when the states are in desperate need for revenue, these excise taxes are no longer generating the funds that they once did. The amount of state revenues generated by excise taxes has decreased from 26 percent in 1972 to 16 percent in 1993 (*New York Times*, 3/2/93, p. B1). The primary reason for this decline in excise tax revenue has been the decline in alcohol and cigarette sales, which have historically been the easiest to raise, in part because the public has accepted the notion that these activities ought to be discouraged. Yet states are still faced with the problem of either raising other taxes, cutting services, or developing a strategy that will enable them to stabilize their excise tax revenues.

In this chapter, we will analyze the revenue issues that states face when they consider raising their cigarette excise tax. In the previous chapter, we also saw how states have developed cigarette excise tax strategies to reduce cigarette sales and how the cigarette firms reacted to these strategies developed by states. But it might very well be possible to increase revenue while decreasing sales if the rate of cigarette excise tax increases makes up for any decrease in cigarette sales. Certainly, the profits of cigarette firms have managed to increase quite handsomely throughout the 1980s and 1990s even though cigarette sales have declined throughout this period.

The question this chapter needs to answer is, Can states increase cigarette tax revenues while decreasing cigarette sales? We will focus on two areas in the formulation and implementation of any possible cigarette excise tax strategy by public policy: forces within the state itself, and forces from outside the state. Like any strategy, a cigarette excise tax strategy must take into account both its "internal" and "external" environments as it tries to stabilize its cigarette excise tax revenue.

INTERNAL ENVIRONMENT: SMALL CONTINUOUS INCREASES VERSUS VERY LARGE INCREASES

Previously, it was concluded that a series of both small and moderate cigarette excise tax increases and one very large excise tax increase had a negative effect on cigarette sales. Now it is time to examine whether these strategies adversely affected cigarette excise tax revenue either over the short or the long term.

We will examine three cases: Rhode Island, Massachusetts, and Washington. All three of these states had implemented a cigarette excise tax strategy that led to a significant decline in cigarette sales. We will now see if any of these states suffered any significant lost of revenue as a result of this decrease in sales. Once again, the statistical analysis (i.e., ARIMA Intervention analysis) of the revenue data will be included at the end of the chapter.

Rhode Island

As the reader might recall, Rhode Island's cigarette excise tax rate has been consistently one of the highest in the United States throughout both the Second and Third Waves of regulation of the cigarette industry. It has raised its cigarette excise tax on a fairly regular basis, with increases usually occurring every three years. Although these frequent increases in the cigarette excise tax were able to "speed up" the rate of decrease in cigarette sales, I will now discuss the effects which these frequent increases had on revenues generated by Rhode Island's cigarette excise tax.

Figure 6.1 shows the trends that Rhode Island's cigarette excise tax revenue had from 1988 to 1994. The ARIMA model that best fits Rhode Island's revenue figures is one in which there has been a slow but steady increase in the revenue stream. In other words, even though cigarette

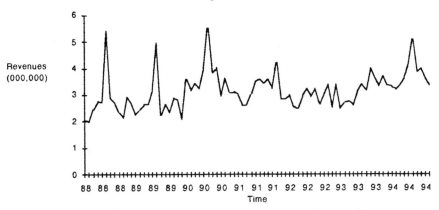

Figure 6.1 Rhode Island's cigarette excise tax revenue (1988 to 1994). *Source:* Adapted from Tobacco Institute

sales have fallen, revenue has risen throughout the period from 1988 to 1994. Rhode Island has been able to keep cigarette excise tax revenue consistent with frequent increases in the excise tax rate to compensate for the decrease in cigarette sales. In many ways, Rhode Island's strategy of frequent low and moderate cigarette excise tax increases appears to be an ideal solution for public policy makers facing the cigarette and health issue. For not only can the state claim that it is helping to discourage cigarette smoking by raising the cigarette excise tax, but the state is also profiting quite consistently from these frequent increases in the excise tax rate. In many ways, Rhode Island appears to be following the pricing policy of the cigarette firms. Small and moderate cigarette excise tax increases are merely added to the price increases to which the cigarette consumers have become quite accustomed. So, just as the cigarette firms seem to be "milking" their customers, public policy makers have joined the cigarette firms in finding cigarette smokers a very lucrative source of revenue.

Massachusetts

In January 1993, Massachusetts almost doubled its cigarette excise tax from 26 cents per pack to 51 cents per pack. It was the first time that Massachusetts had raised its cigarette excise tax in nearly twenty years. Earlier, we saw that cigarette sales fell significantly after the imposition of this increase. We will now investigate whether this increase was so steep as to discourage enough cigarette smokers to quit smoking that revenues actually fell.

Figure 6.2 provides a graphic illustration of how significantly cigarette excise tax revenue rose after the imposition of a large cigarette tax

Figure 6.2 Massachusetts's cigarette excise tax revenue (1988 to 1994). *Source:* Adapted from Tobacco Institute

increase. Although the ARIMA analysis confirms this observation, it also points out that cigarette excise tax revenue had been falling from 1988 to 1992. In others words, the cigarette excise tax rate was too low to compensate for the decrease in cigarette smoking. It certainly appears that public policy makers in Massachusetts missed the opportunity to raise additional funds from cigarette excise tax because they delayed raising this tax earlier. Although the January 1993 increase in the cigarette excise tax rate was quite large, it is doubtful whether it was large enough to make up for the loss of revenue throughout this entire period.

Washington

The state of Washington has traditionally been in the forefront of antismoking strategies. In keeping with this policy, Washington's cigarette excise tax rate has been one of the highest in the nation. In 1987, it had the highest cigarette excise tax rate at 31 cents per pack. In 1990, Washington increased its cigarette excise tax rate to 34 cents per pack. Finally, in July 1993, Washington's cigarette excise tax rate was dramatically raised to 54 cents per pack. Hence, Washington's cigarette excise tax policy is a compromise between the Rhode Island and Massachusetts cigarette excise tax policies. Washington did not raise its cigarette excise tax as often as Rhode Island, nor did it raise its cigarette excise tax as radically as Massachusetts. But this policy did lead to a significant decrease in cigarette sales. We will now examine what effect this cigarette excise tax policy had on cigarette excise tax revenues.

Once again, it is apparent that a large cigarette excise tax increase (of at least 20 cents per pack) has resulted in a very significant increase in revenue (see Figure 6.3). The ARIMA analysis also shows that cigarette

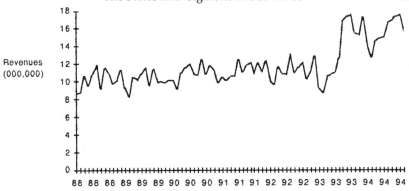

Figure 6.3 Washington's cigarette excise tax revenue (1988 to 1994). *Source:* Adapted from Tobacco Institute

excise tax revenue for the period before July 1993 was for most part stable, especially after the small cigarette excise tax increase of 1990. Washington's cigarette excise tax appears to have been a success on two fronts. It reduced cigarette sales and it produced a consistent source of revenue, although it does appear that, as in the case with Massachusetts, public policy makers could have increased the cigarette excise tax earlier to gain additional revenue and discourage existing or potential cigarette smokers.

CONCLUSION

Overall, it does appear that the cigarette excise tax is a versatile public policy instrument. It can achieve the dual goals of reducing consumption and raising revenue. The ability to raise the cigarette excise tax to quite high levels also shows just how elastic public demand for cigarettes is.

If one combines the results of this chapter with those of the previous chapter, there is little doubt that the cigarette excise tax is the most powerful weapon public policy makers possess in trying to influence the structure of the cigarette industry and raising desperately needed revenue for strapped state budgets. Given these facts, it is remarkable that most states seem to be reluctant to use this public policy instrument. This analysis shows that public policy makers have three strategic options in using the cigarette excise tax: (1) a series of small and moderate increases timed so that as the number of cigarette smokers decline, the excise tax is increased to compensate for any decrease in cigarette sales (Rhode Island has used this strategy quite effectively); (2) a large one-time increase in the cigarette excise tax, which is set high enough to compensate for the loss of cigarette smokers (Massachusetts employed this strategy in 1993); (3) a combination of both of these strategies where there is a small cigarette excise tax increase followed by a large increase (Washington applied this strategic option in setting its cigarette excise tax rate).

It is remarkable that more states have not raised their cigarette excise tax rates more frequently. Perhaps they are afraid that their cigarette-smoking constituents will attempt to purchase their cigarettes in a neighboring state that maintains lower excise tax rates. In the final section of this chapter, I will examine whether or not states that raise their cigarette excise tax rates to a high level actually lose cigarette sales (and hence potential revenue) to a neighboring state.

EXTERNAL ENVIRONMENT: STATES COMPETING FOR CIGARETTE EXCISE TAX REVENUE

One of the major complaints by revenue officials in states that have imposed high cigarette excise tax rates is the amount of "bootlegging" traffic in cigarettes that develops as a result of high cigarette excise tax rates. For example, revenue agents in high cigarette excise tax states such as New Jersey, New York, and Connecticut complain that residents simply cross the border to states with lower taxes. For example, residents of southern New Jersey go to Delaware to buy cigarettes that are taxed at 24 cents per pack, thereby avoiding New Jersey's 40 cents per pack. In addition, Delaware has no sales tax whereas New Jersey has a 6 percent sales tax. Ironically, New Yorkers go to New Jersey to avoid New York's 47 cents per pack as well as taking advantage of New Jersey's lower sales tax. By setting lower excise tax rates and lower sales taxes, states are competing with one another to obtain revenue.

In this section, I will examine the extent to which this "bootlegging" phenomenon is as widespread as state officials contend by analyzing two familiar cases: Massachusetts and Washington. Because both of these states had large cigarette excise taxes increases, if the "bootlegging" thesis holds, neighboring states with lower cigarette excise tax rates ought to have experienced a significant increase in cigarette sales. Obviously, if these neighboring states did experience an increase in cigarette sales, there will be a corresponding increase in cigarette excise tax revenue without having to raise the excise tax on its own cigarette smokers.

Massachusetts and Its Neighbor, New Hampshire

Massachusetts's cigarette excise tax (51 cents per pack) is at least twice the rate of of its neighboring state, New Hampshire (25 cents per pack). Massachusetts officials have long complained about the loss of

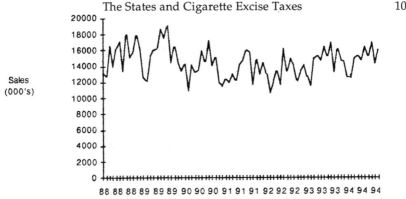

Sales
(000's)

Time

Figure 6.4 New Hampshire's cigarette sales (1988 to 1994). *Source:* Adapted from Tobacco Institute

revenue from "bootlegged" cigarette and alcohol sales. In fact, New Hampshire appears to have directed its own state police to protect Massachusetts residents who buy cigarettes and alcohol in New Hampshire. New Hampshire state police harass undercover Massachusetts state police who sit in parking lots relaying license plate numbers of the cars of Massachusetts residents who are seen buying large quantities of cigarettes and alcohol in New Hampshire.

In this analysis, I will examine whether or not cigarette sales in New Hampshire increased significantly when Massachusetts raised its cigarette excise tax to 51 cents per pack in January 1993.

Figure 6.4 represents cigarette sales from 1988 to 1994 in New Hampshire. The ARIMA Intervention analysis showed that although there was no dramatic one-time increase in New Hampshire's cigarette sales, New Hampshire did experience a gradual long-term increase in sales. It appears that Massachusetts cigarette smokers did not react all at once to the large increase in the cigarette excise tax in Massachusetts. However, if a cigarette smoker in Massachusetts made the decision to continue smoking, some of these Massachusetts cigarette consumers took advantage of much lower cigarette excise taxes and sales taxes in a neighboring state such as New Hampshire.

Washington and Its Neighbor, Oregon

In January 1994, Washington raised its cigarette excise tax from 31 cents per pack to 54 cents per pack. This rate was 16 cents per pack higher than Oregon's cigarette excise tax. Once again, I will examine if

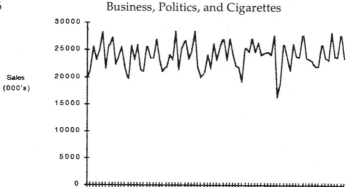

Figure 6.5 Oregon's cigarette sales (1988 to 1994). *Source:* Adapted from Tobacco Institute

cigarette sales in Oregon increased as a result of Washington's dramatic increase in its cigarette excise tax rate.

Oregon's cigarette sales (Figure 6.5) reveal a picture which is very similar to the one we saw for New Hampshire. Once again, the ARIMA Intervention analysis reveals that Oregon did not experience a rapid increase in cigarette sales. Oregon did have a gradual increase in cigarette sales after the imposition of Washington's cigarette excise tax rate increase.

What is even more revealing is that Oregon plans to decrease its cigarette excise tax rate from 38 cents per pack to 28 cents per pack on July 1, 1995, when Washington increases its cigarette excise tax to 75 cents per pack. It appears that Oregon officials think that they can attract enough cigarette smokers from Washington to compensate for the loss of cigarette excise tax from its own cigarette smokers. Perhaps Oregon officials are also trying to keep Oregonian cigarette smokers from crossing the border to buy their cigarettes in Idaho which has a cigarette excise tax rate of only $.18 per pack. It does appear that public officials should be well aware of the financial implications of raising or lowering cigarette excise tax increases.

Conclusion

What the preceding analysis confirms is that states do indeed covet potential cigarette excise tax revenue from neighboring states. Rather than raising their own cigarette excise taxes to raise additional revenue, many states are maintaining or even lowering their cigarette excise tax rate to attract cigarette smokers from neighboring states that have substantially increased their cigarette excise tax rate. In many ways, the states are merely imitating the pricing strategies of the cigarette firms themselves. The cigarette firms can choose either to charge full price for a brand and hope that consumers will pay the higher price out of brand loyalty or to sell generic cigarettes that are discounted to attract price-sensitive consumers. States that substantially raise their cigarette excise tax rates are following a high-price strategy that hopes to "milk" cigarette smokers for additional revenue whereas states that maintain or lower cigarette excise tax rates are hoping to gain market share in a declining market to ensure a future stream of cigarette excise tax income.

Public policy makers face two key questions as they deal with the question of what is the appropriate level for setting their cigarette excise tax rates: (1) Will an excise tax increase substantially reduce the number of cigarette smokers or discourage young smokers from starting the habit? and (2) How will neighboring states react to an increase in the cigarette excise tax? Because the cigarette excise tax still makes substantial contributions to state treasuries in a time of financial trouble, these questions take on additional importance. Many commentators such Gary Becker and Michael Grossman question the viability of cigarette excise taxes as a consistent source of revenue for government at any level (*Wall Street Journal*, August 9, 1994, p. A12). How states and even the federal government balance their revenue concerns with health concerns will determine the role that the cigarette excise tax plays in the future. It certainly appears that revenue concerns will win out with the new Republican legislative majority, but the antismoking movement still has some momentum on its side.

In the last two chapters, we have seen that the cigarette excise tax is the most powerful public policy instrument public policy makers possess. It is an instrument used to achieve two goals simultaneously: reducing cigarette sales and increasing cigarette excise tax revenue. But the problems facing U.S. public policy makers as they regulate the cigarette industry are not unique. Earlier, we saw how U.S. cigarette firms have entered the international cigarette market. The problems facing the relationship between government and cigarette firms have taken on an international dimension. In the next chapter, I will examine how foreign governments are dealing with the problem of revenue versus health concerns. One unique aspect to the international cigarette industry is the more direct role that most foreign governments play in the manufacture and distribution of cigarettes and other tobacco products. This aspect will be examined through a unique case study of the problems facing the Spanish cigarette industry.

ARIMA INTERVENTION ANALYSIS

Large Cigarette Excise Tax Increases and Revenue

Rhode Island. Figure 6.1 (Rhode Island's cigarette excise tax revenues from 1988 to 1994) was identified as an ARIMA $(1,1,0)$ $(0,1,1)_{12}$. The parameters were estimated and found to be statistically significant $(p < .05)$.

$\phi_1 = .5613$ $(t = 2.21)$ $\theta_{12} = .6422$ $(t = 3.38)$

$Q = 24.2$ with 48 degrees of freedom and so the model's residuals are white noise and the tentative model is accepted.

This ARIMA model shows that revenues were increasing throughout the entire period examined. No ARIMA Intervention models were found to be statistically significant.

Massachusetts. The time series of cigarette sales for Massachusetts (Figure 6.2) was identified as an ARIMA $(0,1,1)$ $(0,1,1)_{12}$. Again, regular and seasonal differencing achieved stationarity in the series. The MA parameter was estimated and statistically tested with the following results: $\theta_1 = -.09871$ $(t = -5.02)$; $\theta_{12} = -.1329$ $(t = -2.44)$ and $Q = 17.3$ with 48 degrees of freedom $(p<.01)$. We cannot reject the hypothesis that the residuals form white noise and therefore the model is accepted.

The first dynamic model postulated was

$y_t = \omega \ B \ S_t^{(T)}$

where ω is the level of change parameter. This model is consistent with a hypothesis of an expectation of a sudden and permanent increase in revenue from cigarette excise taxes. The parameter value was: $\omega = 10,097$ $(t = 2.95)$. There was a statistically significant increase in revenue and then the revenue time series again resumed its previous pattern, that is, a slow decrease in revenue from the cigarette excise tax after the imposition of the cigarette excise tax increase.

Washington. The time series of cigarette sales for Washington (Figure 6.3) was identified as an ARIMA $(1,1,1)$ $(1,1,0)_{12}$. Again, regular and seasonal differencing achieved stationarity in the series. The AR and MA parameters were estimated and statistically tested with the following results: $\phi_1 = -.0746$ $(t = -2.01)$, $\theta_1 = -.2312$ $(t = -2.82)$; $\phi_{12} = -.0797$ $(t = -2.56)$ and $Q = 23.6$ with 48 degrees of freedom $(p < .01)$ We cannot reject the hypothesis that the residuals form white noise and therefore the model is accepted.

The first dynamic model postulated was

$$y_t = \omega \, B \, S_t^{(T)}$$

where ω is the level of change parameter. This model is consistent with a hypothesis of an expectation of a sudden and permanent increase in revenue from the cigarette excise tax. The parameter value was $\omega = 7,106$ ($t = 2.93$) As in the case of Massachusetts, there was a statistically significant increase in revenues, and revenue from the cigarette excise tax again resumed its previous pattern before the imposition of the cigarette excise tax increase.

States Competing for Cigarette Excise Tax Revenue

New Hampshire. Figure 6.4 (New Hampshire's cigarette sales from 1988 to 1994) was identified as an ARIMA $(1,1,1)$ $(1,1,1)_{12}$. The parameters were estimated and found to be statistically significant ($p<.05$).

$\varphi_1 = -.1021$ ($t = -2.73$) $\theta_1 = -.0662$ ($t = -2.83$)
$\varphi_{12} = -.2063$ ($t = -2.63$) $\theta_{12} = -.0724$ ($t = -3.04$)

$Q = 24.2$ with 48 degrees of freedom and so the model's residuals are white noise and the tentative model is accepted.
  The first model postulated was

$$y_t = \omega B S_t^{(T)}.$$

The parameter value was $\omega = 724$ ($t = .64$). The permanent impact of the excise tax increase appears to be statistically insignificant. A model was postulated that corresponds to the hypothesis that there was a gradual impact of the cigarette excise tax increase on revenue:

$$y_t = \{ \omega B / (1 + \delta) \} \, P_t^{(T)}$$

with the following results:

$$\omega = 1,058.9 \ (t = .74) \ \delta = .24 \ (t = 3.08).$$

These results indicate that cigarette sales did go up significantly at first and the rate of increase in cigarette sales increased after the imposition of Massachusetts's cigarette excise tax increase.

Oregon. Figure 6.5 (Oregon's cigarette sales from 1988 to 1994) was identified as an ARIMA $(1,1,1)$ $(1,1,0)_{12}$. The parameters were estimated and found to be statistically significant ($p<.05$).

$$\varphi_1 = -.0283 \ (t = -3.72) \quad \theta_1 = -.0473 \ (t = -2.43) \quad \varphi_{-12} = -.0357 \ (t = -3.23)$$

$Q = 22.7$ with 48 degrees of freedom and so the model's residuals are white noise and the tentative model is accepted.

The first model postulated was

$$y_t = \omega BS_t^{(T)}.$$

The parameter value was $\omega = 3,724$ ($t = .93$). The permanent impact of the excise tax increase appears to be statistically insignificant. A model was postulated that corresponds to the hypothesis that there was a gradual impact of the cigarette excise tax increase on revenue:

$$y_t = \{ \omega B / (1 + \delta)\} P_t^{(T)}$$

with the following results:

$$\omega = 2,358 \ (t = .96) \quad \delta = .59 \ (t = 2.78).$$

These results indicate that cigarette sales did go up significantly at first and the rate of increase in cigarette sales increased after the imposition of Washington's cigarette excise tax increase.

Part III
The Future of the Cigarette Industry

New Horizons for the Cigarette Industry: The Privatization of the Worldwide Cigarette Industry

INTRODUCTION

The focus of this book has so far been on the relationship of the U.S. cigarette industry with all levels and branches of government in the United States. In the previous chapter, I examined the effects that various policy measures had on cigarette sales, the pricing of cigarettes, and competition between states for cigarette excise tax revenues. In this chapter, I will analyze the relationship that foreign governments have with their cigarette industries.

Although U.S. cigarette firms dominate the worldwide cigarette industry, their relationship with the U.S. government is rather unique. The U.S. cigarette industry has always been operated by private concerns. In most countries, this is simply not the case. In fact, the production, distribution, and sales of cigarettes are strictly controlled by government agencies. Popular U.S. cigarette brands are "licensed" by governments but in no way are U.S. cigarette firms allowed to operate in the manner in which they operate in the United States. Although they sometimes produce their own brands, they have no control over the distribution and pricing of cigarettes in these foreign markets. Usually, American brands demand premium prices and additional excise taxes. Hence, domestic brands are not only cheaper but also have a lower excise tax. This is one reason why U.S. cigarette firms find that their foreign operations are not nearly as profitable as their U.S. operations. In other words, the huge cash flows that the private U.S. cigarette firms earn go directly into government coffers along with the usual cigarette excise tax revenues. Thus the cigarette industry is an incredibly profit-able operation for most governments throughout the world.

However, the smoking and health issue has forced governments to reconsider their role as producer and distributor of cigarettes. There is an obvious conflict between government agencies that are concerned about the health and welfare of its constituents and those agencies whose charge is to raise funds for government through the production and sale of cigarettes. There are stakeholder groups that have antismok-ing interests, and there are other stakeholder groups that have a clear interest in preserving the cigarette industry and the substantial source of revenue it has become for most governments. Thus, in their dealings with the cigarette industry, public policy makers must balance between the revenue needs of the state and the health concerns of the antismok-ing forces.

PUBLIC POLICY OPTIONS

In dealing with these various stakeholders involved in the cigarette industry, public policy makers have three strategic options. The first option is merely maintaining the status quo. There are two advantages to this option. Obviously, one is economic. The government continues to profit handsomely from cigarette smokers. At the same time, govern-ments, such as France, that have chosen this option can maintain that they can control the production, distribution, and consumption of cig-arettes if they continue the current government monopoly of the ciga-rette industry. Of course, the disadvantage of this option is simply that antismoking groups can maintain that the government cannot direct its full resources and power in conducting antismoking campaigns. As the antismoking groups become stronger, this governmental monopoly of cigarettes becomes increasingly less appealing to public policy makers even if government is willing to use some of the cigarette revenue for antismoking programs.

The two other options that governments have in dealing with their "nationalized" cigarette industries is privatization. This strategy has become quite popular with many governments as they seek to turn to market solutions for their various economic problems. The first way to privatize a cigarette industry is to sell the entire nationalized cigarette enterprise to a foreign firm. The vast majority of these sales will be to be either Philip Morris, RJR, or British Imperial along with other pre-viously nationalized firms. The list of some of the countries that choose this solution include Italy, Hungary, the Czech Republic, Lithuania, Ecuador, and Malaysia.

This solution has two main advantages: first, the huge cash payment for the purchase of the nationalized cigarette firm certainly helps government coffers in the short run; second, the government is free to claim that it no longer encourages the cigarette habit while it still receives substantial cigarette excise tax revenues. But this solution also forces government to face many other questions. With the sale of the government's cigarette monopoly, should the government allow other cigarette manufacturers to compete with the newly privatized cigarette firm? In other words, is privatization merely a transfer of monopoly power from government to private hands or does it signal a truly open market for cigarette smokers? Besides the production monopoly, there also existed a distribution monopoly on cigarettes. Again, the government is faced with the question of whether to permit cigarette sales in certain designated shops or in most retail establishments. Finally, these governments are faced with the question of establishing the appropriate excise tax rate. Antismoking groups will be agitating for extremely high excise tax increases to discourage smoking and there will be a great need to ensure that cigarette excise tax can be maintained. But besides these revenue questions, there is also a question of control of the newly privatized cigarette industry. How much control will the government have over these private cigarette firms in terms of advertising and pricing policies? Will these firms try to entice new smokers through aggressive advertising campaigns? Would these firms establish pricing policies to ensure that smokers will not face any economic pressure to quit smoking? Governments that choose this option will now face the same questions that the U.S. government has faced in dealing with its cigarette industry. In many ways, the exercise of this option is the "Americanization" of the worldwide cigarette industry.

There is, however, another privatization option to be examined. It involves the sale of controlling interest in the nationalized cigarette firm to local businesspersons while government retains a substantial interest in the newly privatized firm. An example of this "partial" privatization occurred in Spain in 1986 when the Spanish government privatized its cigarette firm, Tabacalera. The rest of this chapter will examine this unique example of privatization. To accomplish this task, a model will be developed to help the reader evaluate the success or failure of any privatization scheme.

TABACALERA

Before 1986, Tabacalera's primary market was Spain and other areas where Spanish was primarily spoken. Spain, like most European countries, differentiates its cigarettes by classifying them as *negro* (black) or

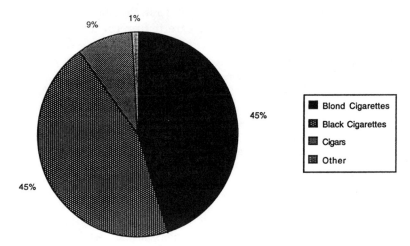

Figure 7.1 1980 market share for each of Tabacalera's tobacco products. *Source: Memoria Tabacalera, S.A.*

rubio (blond). The black cigarettes have a considerably stronger taste and higher nicotine content than the blond or American cigarettes. Whereas the tobacco for making the black cigarettes comes from Turkey, Egypt, and the Spanish Canary Islands, blond cigarettes are made from tobacco grown on the coastal plains of Virginia, Maryland, and North Carolina. Although Tabacalera has several of its own brands of "black" cigarettes, it has contractual agreements with the major international tobacco companies (primarily, Philip Morris and RJR) to manufacture their products (i.e., blond cigarettes) in Spain under license. By examining Figure 7.1, it can be ascertained that cigarettes sales were evenly divided between the traditional "black" cigarette and the newer, blond cigarettes in 1980 (Memoria, 1986).

However, during the 1980s, there were significant changes taking place in the cigarette market. On the positive side (at least as far as Tabacalera was concerned) the sales of cigarettes were to increase during the next seven years by 53.8 percent (Taylor, 1989, p. 57). But new smokers were overwhelmingly choosing blond cigarettes (Marlboro was gathering well over 50 percent of these new smokers during the early 1980s in Spain). Ironically, these new smokers were searching for a "healthy" cigarette and American cigarette producers were well positioned to provide a cigarette for every taste and desire. Tabacalera merely took a slice out of the healthy profits these American cigarettes afforded licensing nationalized cigarette firms. However, Figure 7.2 shows the dramatic shift in market share that had taken place between 1980 and 1987. Tabacalera was forced to make a series of strategic decisions in the

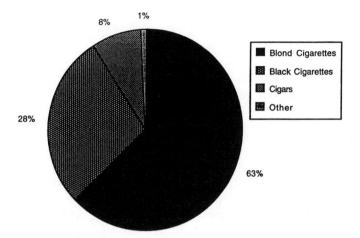

Figure 7.2 1987 market share for each of Tabacalera's tobacco products. *Source: Memoria Tabacalera, S.A.*

early 1980s about how it was going to compete effectively in the future cigarette market. Obviously, in Spain, Tabacalera had a monopoly on the sales of American blond cigarettes in Spain. But with Spain's entry into the European Common Market (EC in what follows), and the lowering of the trade barriers in 1992, Tabacalera faced the challenge of finding ways in which to continue to grow in its cigarettes sales.

There were two options opened to Tabacalera. First, Tabacalera could continue its present policy of licensing American cigarettes and promoting the use of these American blond cigarettes in Spain to ensure its slice of the fastest growing part of the cigarette market. The second option available to Tabacelera was to develop and promote its own brands of blond cigarettes. This was obviously a risky strategy, but if it were successfully implemented it would permit Tabacelera to achieve two goals: (1) it would increase profit margins on its blond cigarette sales substantially since Tabacalera would no longer have to share profits with the American firms; (2) it would permit Tabacalera to enter into the blond cigarette market in other EC countries without being subject to a nationalized cigarette firm's licensing procedure.

But once Tabacalera had decided what its "blond" cigarette strategy was to be, it was now faced with the problem of what to do about its "black" cigarette sales. One option would be to allow this market to die a slow death and milk it for all of the profits that could be obtained. Another might be to give a license to a European cigarette firm in exchange for having that firm sponsor Tabacalera's efforts to get into the blond cigarette market. Finally, an effort could be made to preserve this traditional market by differentiating black cigarettes from blond cigarettes according to price.

The Role of the Spanish Government in the Future Development of Tabacalera

Of course, all of these strategic policies discussed in the previous section were being carried out to please Tabacalera's one and only stockholder, the Spanish government. Because Tabacalera accounted for almost 4 percent of all revenue ($2.5 billion) the Spanish government received in 1984, the performance of Tabacalera was of more than passing interest to the Spanish government. With its entrance into the EC and the impending changes in business and tariff policies in 1992, changes would have to be made in Tabacalera's legal status. Tabacalera's monopoly on wholesale cigarette sales would cease in 1992, and all government interference in the marketing of cigarettes between European competitors was expected to cease. The problem that faced the Spanish government was simply this: What set of policies should it follow to ensure that Tabacalera would continue to grow and prosper so that it could remain a major source of revenue to the Spanish government, as it had been throughout its history, and at the same time satisfy the a growing antismoking movement, which was demanding that government take action to discourage cigarette use.

To meet the legal requirement of entry into the EC, the following act, "31/1985, Monopolio Fiscal de Tabascos," was passed on November 22, 1985. The chief provisions of this act were the following:

1. As of December 31, 1985, the state would sell 48 percent of its interest in Tabacalera and would not interfere in operation of the firm in any manner. Dividends were to be paid to the Spanish government like any other shareholder.
2. The monopoly on the manufacturing of tobacco and on the importing and distributing of non–EC-manufactured tobaccos was to be maintained and exercised by Tabacalera.
3. The wholesale importation and trade of tobacco products by EC firms was now legalized.
4. The Tobacco Rent Tax was abolished, with its fiscal charge being absorbed by the special tax on tobacco and value-added tax so that starting in 1986, tobacco taxation was amortized in accord with the norms of the EC to ensure the principle of nondiscrimination toward tobacco products of other EC members.
5. The government monopoly of retail selling of tobacco products was maintained.

With the passage of this act, Tabacalera had entered into a competitive milieu, fully assuming the risks associated with its activities, which at this point were primarily the manufacturing of tobacco products, mostly cigarettes. Tabacalera had complete control over its own financial future and was free to determine what areas of business it could enter in the future.

Although this act satisfied the EC requirements for Tabacalera, it left one glaring problem for the Spanish government to face. The fourth provision of the 1986 act was the enactment of a value-added tax on tobacco products that was to be in accord with the value-added tax charged by the EC. In other words, the Spanish government could impose an excise tax of any amount it wished on cigarettes at the retail level but it could only tax cigarettes at the wholesale level by a set amount set by the EC. The intention behind the VAT tax was to prevent discrimination against other EC cigarette producers (Castaneda, 1988, p. 186).

There was also one additional force that had to be taken into account before the Spanish government could determine the appropriate excise tax rate on retail cigarettes. In 1986, the Spanish Ministry of Health issued its first statements on the dangers of cigarette smoking. The ministry requested funds from cigarette revenue to finance antismoking programs in Spanish schools. There was also a call by antismoking forces that cigarette advertising be banned from TV and radio. For the first time in Spanish history, antismoking forces were being taken seriously. In fact, by September 1986, the political sentiments against cigarette smoking had grown strong enough to get legislators to enact a smoking ban in public areas such as theaters and buses.

So, in determining what the excise tax rate should be on retail cigarette sales, the Spanish government, like most governments, was faced with the following dilemma: should the excise tax rate be set to ensure that tax revenue to the government is maximized, or should the excise tax be set so high that it will discourage the use of cigarettes to satisfy growing antismoking sentiments? As usual, a compromise was reached that was to go into effect on January 1, 1987. The tax increase was to increase the retail price by 5 percent with the promise of additional increases in the future.

The Spanish government was forced by its commitment to join the EC to give up its some control over its cigarette industry. But in doing so it certainly did not want to give up any revenue that it had access to previously. Obviously, it could still exercise considerable control over Tabacalera not only through its use of excise taxes but also as the majority stockholder in the firm. However, Tabacalera was now a private firm and for the time being in full control of its own destiny. It is also interesting to note that the Spanish government encouraged

Tabacalera to adopt a corporate strategy quite similar to that which has been practiced by American cigarette firms—diversification into related industries.

In this section, the evolution of a public monopoly to a quasi-private firm has been documented. In the next section, the various business strategies that Tabacalera adopted will be discussed. In the final two sections of the chapter, I will evaluate the success of this privatization process of the Spanish cigarette industry.

Tabacalera's Strategic Options

Immediately after Tabacalera gained its independence it decided to enter the blond cigarette market on a full-scale basis. Six months later, it entered the low-nicotine cigarette market because this type of cigarette accounted for over 6.3 percent of all cigarette sales in Spain. Tabacalera also introduced a new blond cigarette brand for women called "Diana." At the same time, Tabacalera doubled the advertising budget of its leading blond cigarette brand, "Fortuna." Most of this increase in Fortuna's advertising budget was given to Tabatrade International, S.A., which had as its aim to promote the exportation of Spanish cigarette products and development of an international trade of Spanish tobacco products.

Tabacalera's black cigarette strategy was twofold. First, Tabacalera decided to release a new black cigarette brand, "Ducados International," which was to be introduced first in France and then throughout the world. Second, Tabacalera decided not to increase prices on black cigarette brands as often as on blond cigarettes and to keep the price of black cigarettes substantially less than the price of blond cigarettes. See Figures 7.3, 7.4, 7.5, and 7.6, which illustrate the extent to which this policy was carried during the period from 1980 to 1988. Two things become quite apparent in Tabacalera's pricing policy: (1) the price of black cigarettes is usually kept at about 35 percent of the price for blond cigarettes; and (2) because blond cigarettes are priced so much higher than black cigarettes, price increases for blond cigarettes seem to occur much more regularly and are much more easily absorbed by the consumer.

Hence, with the passage of Monopolio Fiscal de Tabascos in 1985, the Spanish government permitted Tabacalera to embark upon a very aggressive growth strategy for blond cigarettes and to preserve and maintain its share of the black cigarette market. The marketing of blond cigarettes would resemble very much that of American cigarette firms, which ironically were the chief sources of blond cigarettes for Tabacalera up to that time. Price would be the chief strategic weapon

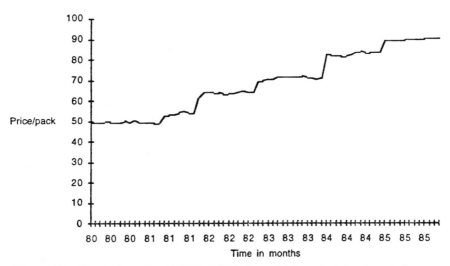

Figure 7.3 Blond cigarettes (1980 to 1985). *Source: Memoria Tabacalera, S.A.*

employed to preserve black cigarette sales. For both types of cigarettes, Tabacalera decided to set up a new division whose chief function was to sponsor exports of Spanish cigarettes to other EC countries and to other regions such as Africa and South America.

In the final two sections of this chapter, we will develop a model for evaluating the privatization process and will use this model to determine the success of Tabacalera's privatization strategy.

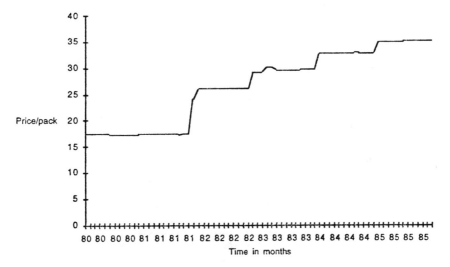

Figure 7.4 Black cigarettes (1980 to 1985). *Source: Memoria Tabacalera, S.A.*

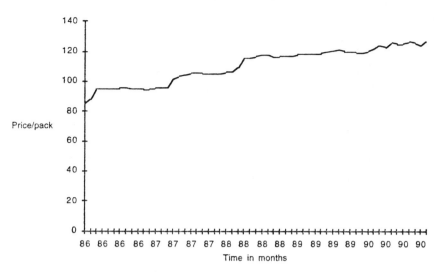

Figure 7.5 Blond cigarettes (1986 to 1990). *Source: Memoria Tabacalera, S.A.*

A FRAMEWORK FOR EVALUATING PRIVATIZATION POLICY

A government's policy decision to privatize a firm or industry that has been traditionally "nationalized" is usually evaluated as to whether economic efficiency has been increased. If the privatization has indeed increased economic efficiency, then it is proclaimed a success (Vickers and Yarrow, 1988).

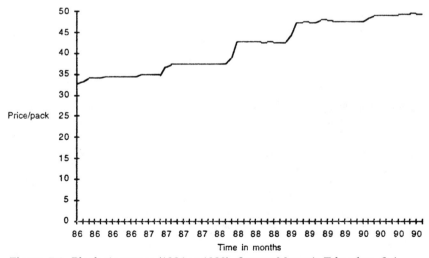

Figure 7.6 Black cigarettes (1986 to 1990). *Source: Memoria Tabacalera, S.A.*

Yet this preoccupation with economic efficiency, particularly in the case of privatization, fails to measure the political consequences that any decision to privatize might have. To deal with this deficiency, Pint (1990, pp. 267–270) has proposed using a "rational-choice" framework "based on the view that interest group members and politicians act as rational decision-makers." It is essentially a cost-benefit analysis that measures both the economic and political consequences for every interest group or stakeholder that will be affected by a proposed privatization. Hence, the real question becomes how to develop a "calculus" that would enable a researcher to calculate the economic and political consequences of a proposed privatization for every interested group.

This would seem to be a daunting task. For even if there could be agreement on what constituted the costs and benefits of any privatization for every stakeholder, these calculations could only be calculated for short-run costs and benefits and would be nearly impossible to estimate for the long-run. However, this distinction between short-run and long-run costs and benefits provides an opportunity to employ both Vicker and Yarrow's emphasis on efficiency and Pint's observation that political consequences must be taken into account in determining the "success" of any privatization policy by government.

The Framework

The purpose of this framework (shown in Figure 7.7) is to provide the reader with a four-step process by which a privatization can be evaluated. The rest of this section will be used to explain how this process works. By necessity, our discussion will begin with a discussion of the short-run criteria, because without short-run success, there certainly will not be any possibility of long-run success!

The first cell (1) of the framework or matrix is concerned with the efficiency that the newly privatized firm or industry displays in the period after it has been privatized. Has privatization enabled the firm or industry to develop business strategies that lead to increases in market share and profits? Is the newly privatized firm or industry better able to achieve operating economies and reduce its overall cost structure? This cell is the primary emphasis of Vicker and Yarrow and no doubt the most fundamental cell. For if the privatization is not successful on economic terms in the short run, then it can have little hope of being successful in the long run either economically or politically.

But economic efficiency must not be the only goal of the short run during the privatization process. There is also a need for political efficiency, which is represented by cell (2). While many political processes are represented as zero-sum games, the privatization process is

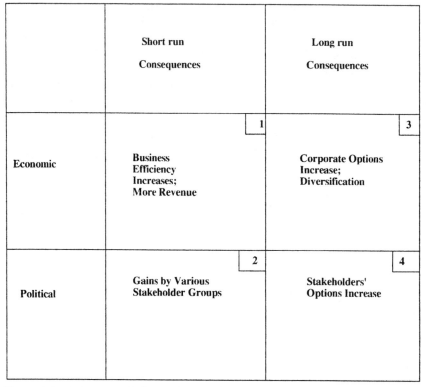

Figure 7.7 A framework for evaluating the privatization process.

certainly not one of them. As Pint (1990, p. 268) has pointed out, the privatization process is quite inefficient if the process is too easily reversed. Therefore, to ensure that the privatization process is efficient, the majority of stakeholders in the privatization process must benefit directly from any privatization of a firm or industry. Government must obtain more revenue (or cut its losses from reduced subsidies) from the newly privatized firm or industry than it received from a nationalized one. Customers must benefit by either receiving a better-quality product/service or paying less for the goods/services that the firm or industry provides. Unions must be reassured that their members will not be the targets of wage cuts or layoffs without some sort of compensation or other assurances given by management. Finally, other interested stakeholders, such as public interest groups and local government, must be satisfied their interests will not be discounted when short-term policy decisions are being made for the newly privatized firm or industry.

The cell (3) represents the long-run economic interests of privatization and has as its goal the development of a corporate strategy that will ensure the continued profitability of the newly created privatized firm or industry. The development of this corporate strategy demands that the privatization process provide the firm or industry with new options in planning its future strategies. Can the firm or industry pursue a diversification strategy so that it is no longer dependent on just one source of revenue? Has privatization enabled the firm or industry to compete in new markets outside those in which it has traditionally been present? Should the privatized firm or industry become vertically integrated either forward or backward? Also, the type of management that is needed to make decisions of this type is not usually found in nationalized or highly regulated firms or industries. It would also seem that for the privatized firm or industry to engage in this sort of long-term corporate strategic thinking, new managers and a new corporate culture would have to be developed. Obviously, if the privatized firm or industry is going to choose any of these corporate strategies, then it must be given the freedom by government to do so. The amount of freedom the government can give to a privatized enterprise is precisely the issue that cell (4) has as its chief concern. Just as the privatized firm or industry needed to have options to establish a basis for long-term economic efficiency, the other stakeholders, which were mentioned in the previous discussion about short-term political efficiency, also need to retain some measure of power or influence over the future course of any previously nationalized firm or industry. For if the privatization process is to be politically viable in the long run, then government must decide the amount of power it will exercise in order to satisfice all the constituencies to which the firm or industry is responsible.

In summary, this framework for evaluating the privatization process requires the evaluator to ask a series of questions about the economic and political effects that the privatization of a firm or industry will have both in the short run and the long run. In the short run, the newly privatized firm or industry not only has to be a modest success economically, but the vast majority of stakeholders also have to perceive that privatization has worked for their betterment. The criterion for long-run success of a privatization is the development of various options for all the stakeholders in the process. This involves having the ability to implement a new corporate strategy for the firm or industry. Meanwhile, government and other stakeholders must maintain a measure of influence in how goals will be set by the privatized firm or industry. The unique feature of this framework is that it recognizes not only the tradeoffs the evaluator must make between the short-run and long-run objectives of privatization, but most importantly the tradeoffs between

the economic and political goals of privatization. For some, nationalization represents the subjugation of economic to political objectives,
whereas privatization can be perceived as the triumph of the economic
goal of efficiency over political concerns about equality. What this
framework is trying to point out is that a privatization cannot be
evaluated correctly unless proper attention is paid to both the economic
and political compromises that must be made if the privatization is to
take place.

The preceding framework will now be used to evaluate the process
by which Tabacalera and the Spanish government hope to make
Tabacalera a successful and profitable private enterprise.

EVALUATING THE PRIVATIZATION
OF TABACALERA

Throughout this analysis, the principal stakeholders whose interest
we consider are Tabacalera, the Spanish government, cigarette consumers, and various antismoking groups. Although there are other groups
such as the media (newspapers, TV, radio) that also have a stake in this
industry, their interest in the privatization of the cigarette industry
would at best be fairly small. Each cell of the four-cell framework will
be examined with particular attention paid to each of these stakeholders.

Cell (1): Evaluating the Short-run Effectiveness of
Tabacalera's Business Strategies

In the previous section, we saw how the relationship between the
Spanish government and Tabacalera, its wholly owned tobacco subsidiary, had changed for two reasons: (1) the change in the type of cigarette
that Spaniards preferred to smoke; (2) Spain's entry into the EC. To deal
with these changes in market and the type of ownership the EC would
permit, the Spanish government "privatized" Tabacalera. The privatization of Tabacalera satisfied the EC requirements and it also permitted
Tabacalera to pursue business policies that would allow Tabacalera to
greatly expand its blond cigarette operations while maintaining its
black cigarette market. In this section, I will analyze just how successful
these business policies were.

Tabacalera's Expansion into the Blond Cigarette Market. As Figures 7.8
and 7.9 clearly demonstrate, the trend for blond cigarette sales sold by
Tabacalera was certainly increasing throughout the period of 1979 to
1988. But the interesting point is that the rate of increase of sales stayed

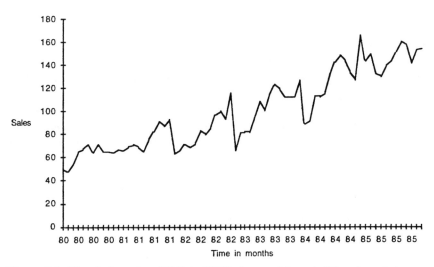

Figure 7.8 Blond cigarettes (1980 to 1985). *Source: Memoria Tabacalera, S.A.*

constant at about 4 percent per year. Two things can be inferred from this development. First, Tabacalera's steps to enter the blond cigarette market have been steady but hardly spectacular. Tabacalera has followed the American cigarette producers' lead of creating a cigarette for every niche market. This "follower" strategy has enabled Tabacalera not only to enter its own blond cigarette market but also to cut into the rate of increase in sales of American cigarettes in Spain. However,

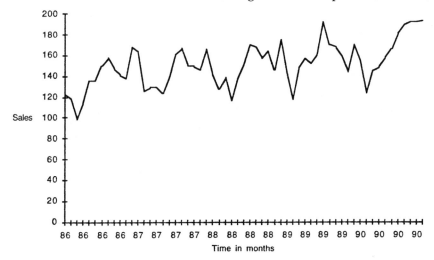

Figure 7.9 Blond cigarettes (1986 to 1990). *Source: Memoria Tabacalera, S.A.*

Tabacalera's success in exporting these blond cigarette brands to other markets has been only moderately successful. Of course, one cannot forget that Tabacalera's development of these various blond cigarette brands will give it a competitive advantage in competing for the 1992 EC market. The other conclusion one can draw from this constant growth of blond cigarette sales is that the cigarette excise tax increase had no effect on blond cigarette sales. For a more rigorous statistical analysis of this sales data (ARIMA Intervention analysis), please see McGowan (1989). Overall, Tabacalera's blond cigarette strategy has been a success in establishing a domestic market and gaining a foothold in the potentially lucrative export market.

Tabacalera's Pricing Strategy for Maintaining Black Cigarette Sales. Tabacalera's strategy for its black cigarette sales seems to be centered on preserving its market and revenue for a product whose life cycle seems to be ending. The price of these cigarettes was kept much lower than that for blond cigarettes even though the cost for making these kinds of cigarettes was nearly identical. Tabacalera was also trying to establish an export market for these cigarettes.

From Figures 7.10 and 7.11, it is clear that this "holding" strategy was not successful. Despite making black cigarettes significantly cheaper than blond cigarettes, black cigarette sales continued to decline at about 3 percent per year in the period 1979 to 1988. How successful Tabacalera will be in establishing an export market for black cigarettes remains to

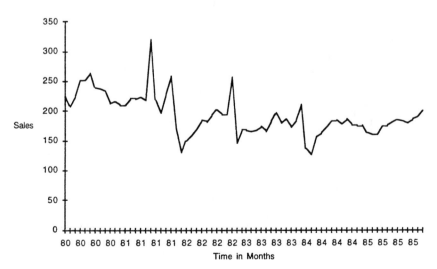

Figure 7.10 Black cigarette sales (1980 to 1985) *Source: Memoria Tabacalera, S.A.*

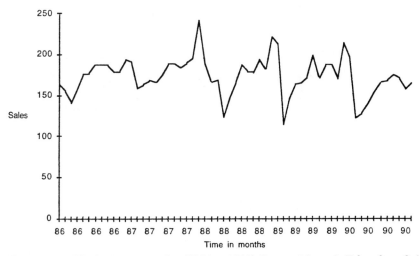

Figure 7.11   Black cigarette sales (1986 to 1990) *Source: Memoria Tabacalera, S.A.*

be seen. But even it proves to be successful the revenue this product can generate will not be very substantial because younger smokers through-out the world have shown a clear preference for blond cigarettes. As was the case with blond cigarettes, we can also ascertain that the excise tax increase of 1987 had little effect on black cigarette sales. Black cigarette sales did not decline at a faster rate owing to the imposition of this tax. Again, for a rigorous statistical analysis of this data, see McGowan (1989).

Overall, Tabacalera's strategy has failed to increase black cigarette sales although a case could be made that this new strategy at least prevented the decline of black cigarette sales from taking place at an even faster pace. Given the fact that sales have been declining for the past twenty years, there is little doubt that the black cigarette is a dying product and the only real question for Tabacalera is how it can grace-fully exit this market.

Cell (2): Short-run Impact of Privatization on Government and Other Stakeholders

Economists have traditionally maintained that excise taxes can have a dual purpose: to raise revenue for government and to discourage the use of the product or service that is being taxed. From the two previous sections, it is fairly evident that the 1987 Spanish cigarette excise tax increase had no effect on either blond or black cigarette sales. In fact, because overall cigarette sales increased throughout this period, it is not

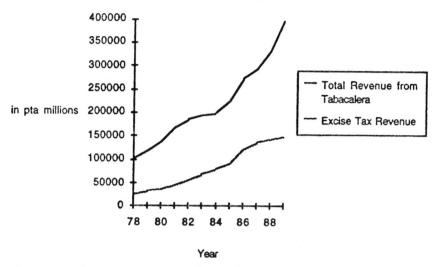

Figure 7.12 Government revenue from Tabacalera. *Source: Memoria Tabacalera, S.A.*

surprising that cigarette excise tax revenues have increased by 22 percent since 1986.

Figure 7.12 makes it apparent that the total revenue (this includes excise taxes, corporate taxes, dividends, and rents on factories) that the Spanish government, receives from Tabacalera's operations has increased by 32 percent since 1986. In 1986, the cigarette excise tax revenue accounted for nearly 48 percent of the total revenue received by the Spanish government, whereas in 1989 the cigarette excise tax accounted for only 32 percent of the total revenue. It is ironic that while cigarette excise tax revenue increased after the privatization of Tabacalera, its importance to the Spanish government as a source of revenue has decreased in relative terms! Dividends, corporate taxes, and rents now account for over 68 percent of the revenue the Spanish government receives from Tabacalera. It is quite apparent that at least in terms of revenue the privatization of Tabacalera has been an overwhelming success. This excise tax increase also permitted the Spanish government to mollify its antismoking critics. It was pointed out during the passage of the excise tax increase that the government was much more willing to increase excise taxes because it was no longer the majority owner of the cigarette firm!

Overall, in the short run, the privatization of Tabacalera was a quite a success. Sales and overall revenue increased significantly and the business policies that were instituted positioned Tabacalera to make additional gains in the international cigarette market. Consumers now had many more brands to choose from and older smokers of black cigarettes were being subsidized by younger smokers of blond cigarettes. The Spanish government was actually receiving more revenue from this newly privatized firm than it received from its nationalized firm. Finally, the growing antismoking movement in Spain was able to establish the excise tax as a weapon in its fight to decrease cigarette smoking. In the next two cells, the long-run consequences of this privatization of the Spanish cigarette industry will be analyzed.

Cell (3): Long-run Economic Consequences of Tabacelera Privatization

It was shown earlier that Tabacalera's aggressive pricing and export policy was successful for establishing itself in the blond cigarette market but was a failure in preserving its traditional black cigarette market. But what was most interesting to note was the strategic behavior of this newly "privatized" firm. In essence, Tabacalera's business strategy for promoting cigarette sales was even more aggressive than that practiced by American cigarette firms because Tabacalera took advantage of the potential export market much more than its American counterparts. In fact, Tabacalera's corporate strategy is exactly like its American counterparts. In 1988, Tabacalera purchased from RJR Nabisco its operations in Spain. Tabacalera, like its American cousins, has invested its excess capital from its cigarette revenues into other food operations. This diversification strategy of Tabacalera has a blessing from the Spanish government much like the American government has seemed to bless Philip Morris's takeovers of Miller Beer, General Foods, Kraft Foods, and Suchard. In 1986, 91 percent of Tabacalera's profits are tobacco related but, much like its American cousins, Tabacalera has not found the diversification strategy particularly successful. But also like its American cousins this march toward diversification seems to be able to deflect some of the political heat for being primarily a "cigarette firm," especially when the largest shareholder happens to be the host government.

Cell (4): Long-run Political Consequences of Tabacalera's Privatization

Certainly, the corporate policy of diversification has pleased antismoking forces because it seems to signal that Tabacalera intends to exit the cigarette business in the long run. But there is little doubt that this measure alone would satisfy the ever-growing agenda of the antismoking forces. However, with the privatization of Tabacalera, the Spanish government has been in a much better position to respond to the demands of these antismoking forces. In 1988, various antismoking bans in the workplace and various public places were enacted to protect nonsmokers from the nuisance and probable health risks of passive smoking. Finally, in 1990, the Spanish parliament passed an act which made TV and radio cigarette advertising illegal in Spain, and there is currently a movement to outlaw cigarette advertising in the print media as well. It seems to be the case that the Spanish government was able to take both a stronger antismoking stance and a quicker action after it divested itself of its direct tobacco interest.

The long-term implications of Tabacalera's privatization appear to have benefited all of the major stakeholders. Economically, the firm has begun to diversify so that it is no longer totally dependent on cigarette sales for revenue and appears to be in a very good position to take full advantage of foreign markets in 1992. Politically, the antismoking forces have been able to prod the Spanish government into enacting much of its legislative agenda. Clearly, the Spanish government has done well financially while doing "good" with its social agenda.

CONCLUSION

The privatization of Tabacalera can be deemed a success. In the short run, the newly privatized Tabacalera was able to develop business strategies that enabled it to increase sales and revenues substantially. Privatization has also permitted Tabacalera to develop a long-run diversification strategy that might allow it to reduce its dependence on its cigarette revenues, but given the profitability of cigarettes, this hardly seems likely, at least in the short-term future. In the political arena, every stakeholder has gained something. While increasing its total revenues, the Spanish government no longer had the political burden of directly controlling this controversial firm, and antismoking forces gained passage of an excise tax increase, numerous anti–public smoking laws, and an advertising ban.

In general, this appears to have been an easier way of privatizing a nationalized cigarette firm than merely selling it off to the highest private bidder. The Spanish government is in a position to receive long-term economic rewards from a successful operation of Tabacalera and future increases in excise tax revenues. Although it can be criticized for being the major beneficiary of a business whose goals conflict with some of its other public policy goals, the Spanish government can claim that it exercises much greater control over Tabacalera's cigarette business because it is the largest single stockholder. This quasi-privatization of the Spanish cigarette industry has enabled the Spanish government to reap extensive economic profit while maintaining substantial control over the industry.

The Spanish government, however, will continue to face a question that the U.S. government has had to face throughout its history: the classical dilemma of whether the rights or freedom of the individual or corporation should prevail over the needs of society. In this case, the Spanish government has taken, for the near term at least, the stance of the American government (i.e., what is good for business is good for the nation). Whether European governments are willing or able to take this stance on privatization only time will tell, but the controversy surrounding the cigarette industry will be with public policy makers for the foreseeable future.

Conclusions, Analysis, and Implications

INTRODUCTION

The conclusion of this book on the cigarette industry will contain two sections: first, the summary of the consequences (both intended and unintended) the Third Wave of public policy measures has had on the cigarette industry and on the other stakeholders that are involved in the "cigarette smoking" issue set; second, the implications of these results not only for the cigarette industry but also other industries that are intimately involved in the Business and Public Policy processes.

The first section of this chapter will present a synopsis of the hypotheses tested in Chapters 4, 5, and 6 along with the implications of these results for the various groups and issues that constitute the smoking and health issue set. To accomplish this task, this section will be broken up into three parts based on the Convergence Model of Business and Public Policy (Figure 3.2, p. 53). In the first part, the effectiveness of the public policy measures intended to decrease cigarette sales will be examined. Both the intended and unintended effects will be analyzed. The implications of these results for the cigarette industry and the firms that make up that industry will be the topic of discussion for the second part of this first section. Finally, the relationship between the public policy process and the various stakeholder groups concerned with the smoking and health controversy will be the topic for examination in the third part of this first section.

The second section of this chapter will examine the implications of these results for the future of the cigarette industry both in the United States and throughout the world. Government's duel interest in the future of the cigarette industry will be discussed both as a U.S. and a worldwide phenomenon.

CONSEQUENCES OF THE THIRD WAVE'S PUBLIC POLICY MEASURES ON THE "SMOKING AND HEALTH" ISSUE SET

Public Policy Measures and Cigarette Sales

The results from Chapters 4 and 5 indicate that only a very substantial increase in the cigarette excise tax rate (of least 20 cents per pack) produced a permanent and lasting decrease in cigarette sales. If the intended goal of public policy makers is *primarily* to decrease cigarette sales, other measures such as advertising bans and smoking bans are merely helpful in promoting an antismoking culture since they were found to be ineffective in reducing cigarette sales.

This finding that only a very substantial increase in the cigarette excise tax rate produces a decrease in cigarette sales would hardly be revolutionary in itself. But with the coming of the Third Wave of regulation and its accompanying increased state involvement in smoking and health issues, the cigarette excise tax becomes the most potent weapon in the antismoking arsenal, although the passage of antismoking prohibitions signals to stakeholders that states are truly interested in discouraging cigarette smoking. The six states whose monthly cigarette sales were studied using ARIMA Intervention analysis represented a wide spectrum of possible policies that states could enact in trying to reduce cigarette smoking. Various possible combinations of excise tax and smoking prohibition policies were examined and it was found that only those states with high cigarette excise tax rates and moderate to high antismoking laws were successful in permanently lowering cigarette consumption. This high cigarette excise tax rate could be achieved either by frequently raising the cigarette excise tax (e.g., Rhode Island) or by enacting a large increase of at least 20 cents per pack (Massachusetts and Washington).

So far, I have examined only one of the *intended* effects these public policy measures had on the cigarette industry and the various stakeholders who have an interest in this industry; it is now time to examine some of the unintended effects of these measures.

Public Policy Measures and the Cigarette Industry

This section will have as its major focus the effects that the various public policy measures of the Third Wave have had on strategies of the cigarette firms and the industry as a whole. These "results" will be characterized as *unintended* because public policy makers were in no position to predict the consequences of their actions on the strategies of the cigarette firm and structure of the cigarette industry other than their *intended* goals of trying to reduce the level of cigarette smoking or raising revenue. To account for these unintended effects in a more systematic fashion, this section will be broken up into two parts: the firm and the industry level.

Firm. The strategy of the individual cigarette firm can also be subdivided into two different levels: product, and business and corporate. I will now explore the unintended effects that the passage of excise tax increases, advertising bans, and smoking bans had on the strategies of the cigarette firms at any of these levels.

Product Level. An integral part of any firm's product strategy is its pricing policy. In Chapter 5, we saw how increases in the cigarette excise tax rate influenced the pricing policies of the cigarette firms. Once again, various cases had to be examined to account for not only the different levels of state excise tax rates (high or low) but also the types of excise tax increases that could be imposed (i.e., a small excise tax increase of 10 cents per pack or less or a large increase of more than 20 cents per pack). Three cases were examined: the effect of a small excise tax increase on cigarette pricing policy; the effect of a moderate excise tax increase on cigarette pricing policy; and the effect of a large excise tax increase on cigarette pricing policy.

The results of this analysis were mixed. When a small or moderate excise tax increase was levied, it appears that the cigarette firms did indeed behave in the manner Harris proposes: these firms implemented price increases that ignored these small excise tax increases. However, this was not the case with large excise tax increases at the state level where it is apparent that the cigarette firms are quite sensitive to large excise tax increases and do refrain from raising their prices when a large increase is imposed. Thus, the imposition of a large cigarette excise tax increase results not only in a decrease in cigarette sales but also has the unintended effect of decreasing the profit that the cigarette firms can attain by holding down price increases.

Business and Corporate Level. One overwhelming conclusion that can be drawn from the analysis presented so far is that the cigarette excise tax, if applied in large enough "doses," can have tremendous intended and unintended effects on the cigarette industry. Although we have seen that the other measures (advertising bans, smoking bans) are not effective in reducing cigarette sales, a case can be made that they are useful to the antismoking forces, particularly smoking bans, to the extent that they do create an antismoking climate or "ideology." This results of this antismoking ideology are most easily observed in the behavior of the cigarette firms at the business and corporate levels of strategic planning.

In Chapter 2, it was shown that one feature characterizing the behavior of the cigarette firms was their desire to expand their share of the international market even though the profit margins in these markets in no way approach the profit margins that can be achieved through the sale of cigarettes in the U.S. market. It is clear to these firms that the American cigarette market is a declining one because of the antismoking culture that has developed in the United States and the future of this industry appears to lie in foreign markets.

The corporate strategies of these firms has also been affected by this antismoking ideology. Since the inception of the smoking and health issue in 1964, "diversification"—usually into related food and beverage products has characterized the corporate strategy of all six cigarette firms. Although it was demonstrated in Chapter 2 that this policy has not been overwhelmingly successful, at least in terms of percentage of profits that these nontobacco sales contribute to the bottom line, this policy does indicate once again that the cigarette firms view their long-run future in marketing consumer goods other than cigarettes.

Besides the creation of an antismoking ideology, these public policy measures have also had other unintended effects, particularly on the structure of the cigarette industry, which is the topic to which we will now turn.

Industry. Because the Convergence Model of Business and Public Policy used Porter's model for industry analysis, this section will be divided according to the various forces (entry and exit barriers, substitute products, customers, and suppliers) that are described in that model. This way of proceeding ought to enable the reader to have a clear understanding of what some of the unintended consequences that the various public policy initiatives had on the structure of the cigarette industry were.

Exit and Entry Barriers. Although none of the public policy measures directly prohibits entry of other firms into this still rather profitable industry, there have been no new entrants into the industry since 1924. There are, of course, various reasons for this phenomenon. It would take at least a year to purchase and cure the tobacco necessary to manufacture cigarettes. There is also an economies-of-scale issue insofar as the investment necessary to compete with the major firms is quite steep; for example, a one-billion-dollar plant completed by RJR in 1986 is capable of producing enough cigarettes for RJR's domestic customers (*Business Week*, 7/4/94, p. 29). But given the level of profits this industry achieves even in the face of declining sales and the prospect of increasing foreign sales, the cigarette industry might seem to be an attractive one to enter.

One might argue that no firm wants to enter an industry whose product has such a negative connotation. The recent announcement by Surgeon General Koop that "cigarette smoking is as addictive as heroin or cocaine" would certainly dissuade a firm from entering this industry (*New York Times*, 12/6/93, p. D1). But even before the advent of this extremely negative publicity, no firm had tried to enter this industry, and in fact, the smaller firms in this industry seem to be getting squeezed out of their already small market share. In the cigarette industry, it appears that the rich are getting richer and the poor are getting poorer. What has caused this phenomenon? One explanation that seems quite plausible is that it is an unintended effect of the TV and radio advertising ban of 1971.

In Chapter 2, it was pointed out that well over 200 brands of cigarettes have been introduced into the U.S. cigarette market since 1964 trying to sell the "healthy" cigarette. Yet we have also seen that none of these new brands have been very successful in capturing even 5 percent of the market (*Business Week*, 7/4/94, p. 25). Meanwhile, established brands, such as Marlboro, are increasing their market share so that in 1994 Marlboro had nearly 22 percent of the total U.S. cigarette share by itself even though there are over 200 brands of cigarettes available to the cigarette smoker.

So while it appears that the advertising ban had no effect on cigarette sales, it did have the unintended effect of making entry into this market virtually impossible because firms could no longer reach smokers through mass media outlets but instead had to concentrate on print media and free samples to introduce new brands. Obviously, these methods have proven to be far inferior to using TV and radio.

In regard to exit barriers, ironically, the chief one seems to be the level of profits that the cigarette firms obtain each year. The cigarette manufacturers stay in the industry because they cannot afford to exit it, hoping that they can use the cigarette profits to finance diversification into other consumer product industries, none of which, however, are nearly as profitable as cigarettes. Hence, the amount of loyalty a firm has to the cigarette industry is correlated to the level of profits that a firm has achieved. Philip Morris and RJR have the greatest stake in the industry, and the other four firms have commitments corresponding to the level of profits they obtain from their cigarette business.

Thus the unintended effect of the various public policy measures, especially the TV and radio advertising ban, on the structure of the cigarette industry has been the creation of a duopsony. The two largest cigarette firms keep increasing their share of a smaller market for cigarettes because entry into the market has been effectively blocked. There are no exit barriers except that the firms are still extremely dependent on cigarette profits to finance entry into other, less controversial industries. Essentially, the cigarette firms are playing a zero-sum game in which the winners are slowly driving the losers out of an industry that all of the firms would like to eventually exit.

Substitute Products. Substitute products for cigarettes are directly related to the smoking and health issue. In the 1960s, the filter cigarette was certainly a substitute product for the traditional nonfilter cigarette, so that by 1970, no nonfiltered cigarette was even in the top fifteen cigarette brands (*Business Week*, 12/26/86, p. 66). In September 1987, RJR introduced a new substitute product called Premier intended to replace the filter cigarette that was being called the "smokeless" cigarette (*New York Times*, 11/29/94, p. D20). This technological development is a logical continuation of the search for the "healthy" cigarette, which began in the 1960s. However, Premier was termed a failure when it bombed its taste tests. But RJR has refused to give up its hope of finding "the healthy cigarette." Recently, RJR introduced a cigarette, Eclipse, that delivers smoke only to the smoker while sparing the nonsmoker. Just how successful this product will be remains to be determined (ibid.).

Yet it appears that history is repeating itself with the introduction of this new substitute product. Once again, Philip Morris is permitting RJR to take the lead in introducing a new product, even though it is believed that Philip Morris also possesses the technology to manufacture this "smokeless" cigarette. PM seems to be more than willing to let RJR do the "spade" work necessary to introduce this new product and is willing to take the risk that it can introduce a brand that will eventually outsell RJR's brand. In the early 1970s, PM's filtered entry, Marlboro, eventually surpassed RJR's filtered entry, Winston, even though Winston had been introduced three years previously. Whether PM can repeat this success story in the antismoking environment of the 1980s, especially if a total ban on all cigarette advertising is enacted, is an interesting question.

Overall, the effect of a substitute product seem to reinforce the effects that the entry and exit barriers had on the structure of the cigarette industry, namely, the creation of a duopsony in which the two leading firms will dominate the introduction of the new product and further reinforce their dominant positions in the cigarette industry.

Customers. It has been shown throughout the history of the cigarette industry that demand for its product is relatively inelastic, and therefore customers have very little power over the pricing policies of the cigarette firms unless the firms intend to impose a huge price increase of more than 10 percent. But what has changed during the course of the Second and Third Waves are the demographics of cigarette smokers.

The typical smoker is no longer a young white male trying to assert his manhood. Rather, the vast majority of new smokers are either women, low income, from a minority group, a newly arrived immigrant or from south of the Mason-Dixon line (*Philadelphia Inquirer*, 7/2/90, p. 5). These changes in the demographics of smoking will have a profound impact on both the strategies of the cigarette firms and public policy makers.

For the cigarette firms, these changes in the characteristics of the typical smoker pose two problems. First, the new cigarette smoker is likely to be much more price sensitive because (s)he comes from a lower income bracket. Therefore, future price increases have to be held down in order not to lose smokers to generic brands. We have already seen the role that excise taxes can play in discouraging cigarette sales. The second change concerns promotional activity. Throughout the 1980s and the 1990s, Philip Morris has led the way in demonstrating how cigarette firms can target markets for its promotional activities. There are various examples of this sort of activity: Virginia Slims tennis and golf tournaments are sponsored for women, and PM also stages numerous black art and music festivals (*New York Times*, 6/24/94, p. D8). These promotional activities serve a dual purpose for Philip Morris: PM gains corporate "respectability" while at the same time reaching a public that is much more likely to smoke cigarettes. Just how successful this type of activity will be in the future also remains to be seen.

For public policy makers, the "new" smoker poses some interesting public policy dilemmas. If the typical smoker is indeed a blue-collar worker, foreign born, and does not work in an office, the effectiveness of smoking prohibition laws is at best suspect because most of these laws are meant to cause discomfort to a typical middle-class cigarette smoker. For although cigarette smoking seems to be have been made unacceptable behavior in white-collar circles, it is still quite acceptable behavior for low-income, blue-collar, foreign-born workers. If policy makers turn to their most effective measure to discourage smoking, the excise tax, the old charge by cigarette firms that excise taxes are regressive seems to have become much more persuasive in the 1990s. For indeed, the average income of smokers has fallen and so any increase in cigarette excise taxes would seemingly add to the tax burden of people who can least afford to pay additional taxes. Although the cigarette excise tax certainly permits government at all levels "to do good while doing well," it also opens government to the charge that it is playing "Robin Hood in reverse" by taking from the poor to balance the government's deficit.

It is time to examine the force that the cigarette industry used to fight these measures to discourage smoking: its alliance with its suppliers.

Suppliers. Throughout its history, the cigarette firms and the small tobacco farmers of the Piedmont plain regions (Maryland, South Carolina, North Carolina, Tennessee, Kentucky, and Virginia) have formed a natural alliance based on their common economic interest—the growing of tobacco and the subsequent production of cigarettes. Hence, it is somewhat ironic that just when the cigarette industry is facing its sternest test from antismoking forces, this alliance between tobacco growers and cigarette producers seems to be coming apart. Two reasons can be given as causes of this development: the imports of tobacco and the drive by cigarette firms to become low-cost producers.

With the development of the filtered cigarette, the quality of tobacco used in manufacturing cigarettes could be lowered. Because filtered cigarettes account for well over 90 percent of all cigarette sales, cigarette firms were on the prowl for a source of lower-quality, cheaper tobacco. (It is ironic that development of the filtered cigarette has also contributed to the profit margins of the cigarette firms.) Imported tobacco, especially from Brazil and Egypt, fulfils these conditions. Sales of imported tobacco have increased substantially since 1964 although the actual usage of these imports cannot be exactly ascertained because it is proprietary information. However, it has led to representatives from the U.S. tobacco-growing states demanding high tariffs on imported tobacco as a means of forcing the cigarette firms to use domestic tobacco. This controversy over imported tobacco was the first crack to develop in the political alliance between the cigarette industry and the congressional delegation from Tobacco Road.

Another factor that led to the deterioration of the cigarette industry's relationship with the Tobacco Road congressional delegations is the drive by most firms in the industry to make their manufacturing plants more efficient. RJR cut its labor force by over 40 percent and doubled cigarette production when it opened its new, fully automated Winston-Salem plant in September 1986 (*Business Week*, 5/3/93, p. 132). Philip Morris and the other cigarette firms have also overhauled old plants and made them much more efficient, thereby reducing the amount of labor needed to manufacture cigarettes.

So although the cigarette firms have undertaken two policies that have greatly increased their profit margins on cigarette sales, the price that they have had to pay for these actions is a loosening of the political ties between the Tobacco Road delegation and themselves. As the economic contribution that the cigarette industry makes to this region continues to fall, so does the political loyalty of the Tobacco Road delegation to the cigarette industry. The industry still has its staunch supporters from the region as typified by Jesse Helms of North Carolina, but other members of this delegation, such as Charles Robb of Virginia, have completely broken with the industry and are willing to support not only smoking prohibition laws but even go as far as supporting cigarette excise tax increases. Indeed, with the coming of the Third Wave and the industry's drive to "milk its cash cow," it is apparent that a "New Politics of Tobacco" has evolved.

THE NEW POLITICS OF TOBACCO: THE CONVERGENCE OF BUSINESS AND PUBLIC POLICY

Figure 8.1 implies that the chief difference between the "Old Politics of Tobacco" and the "New Politics of Tobacco" lies in the perceived

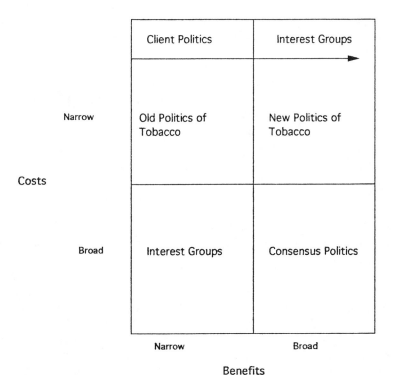

Figure 8.1 New politics of tobacco. *Source:* Adapted from James Q. Wilson, "The Politics of Regulation," pp. 357–394.

benefits to society. With the coming of the "passive smoking" issue and its subsequent development of an antismoking ideology, no longer are the benefits of the antismoking movement confined to a narrow group (the health of cigarette smokers) but rather to society as a whole. We have also seen that the cost to society (the economic contribution of cigarettes to society) is actually narrowing further as the cigarette firms themselves are trying to become less dependent on tobacco, leaving the cost to a smaller and smaller segment of the population—the tobacco farmers on "Tobacco Road."

The rest of this section will be spent examining the problems and opportunities the "New Politics of Tobacco" presents for the various groups or stakeholders involved in the smoking and health issue set: government, the cigarette industry, and antismoking groups.

Government

With the coming of the "New Politics of Tobacco" and its accompanying Third Wave of regulation, the level of government whose role has changed most drastically is the state and local governments' attitude toward cigarette smoking. The federal government's role in the antismoking movement is still beset with contradictions. Although the Surgeon General has labeled cigarette smoking as dangerous as any drug addiction problem, the Department of Agriculture still pushes for subsidies for tobacco farmers. The role that the Judiciary plays in the antismoking movement has been essentially the same in both the Second and Third Waves of regulation. Liability lawsuits are still being filed against the cigarette firms, but the likelihood that one of these suits will result in a substantial judgment against a cigarette firm seems to becoming more and more remote (*New York Times*, 12/6/93, p. D1).

However, the role of the states in passing comprehensive antismoking programs seems to be gaining momentum throughout the country, particularly north of the Mason-Dixon line. Yet there are two problems states face when they try to enact these programs that legislators ought to take into account before taking action.

The cigarette excise tax has proven to be the most effective measure in decreasing cigarette sales, but its value as a weapon to prevent smoking could eventually conflict with its value to the state as a source of revenue. In Chapter 6, we examined the various strategies that states used to ensure that the cigarette excise tax remain a consistent source of revenue. It certainly appears that certain states with high cigarette excise tax rates were willing to reap all of the "short-run" profit while it is available to them. Meanwhile, it was shown how some of the neighboring states were quite content to lure cigarette smokers from these "high" excise tax states. Therefore, it is quite conceivable in the future that a state could actually lose revenue if it raised its excise tax too high. Thus, it does seem that in the future many states will be forced to choose between the public health objective of stopping cigarette smoking and the need to raise revenue through the cigarette excise tax.

Antismoking groups face the revenue and regionalization questions in their efforts to get state legislatures to enact their legislative programs. I will now discuss the problems faced by the cigarette industry as it attempts to deal with the New Politics of Tobacco.

Cigarette Industry

The New Politics of Tobacco and the Third Wave in general pose many threats to the cigarette industry. The one that has received the most attention in this study has been the change in enacting public policy measures from the federal to the state level of government. This development of more state involvement in the antismoking crusade has led to two major changes in the way the cigarette industry has had to deal with antismoking legislation. First, no longer can the cigarette industry concentrate its efforts at the national level. The industry now has to set up outposts to lobby for its interests at every level of government throughout the United States. No longer can it expect that the Tobacco Road congressional delegation can protect its vital interest.

This shift in the level of agenda for antismoking legislation has also compounded the industry's "legitimacy" problem. On the national level, the industry uses two arguments (the implications of the ethical arguments will be discussed in greater detail later) to make its case: first, a person's right to choose if (s)he wants to smoke; second, the enormous economic benefits which the cigarette industry contributes to the economy. Before 1985, the basic ethical argument that antismoking groups used against the cigarette industry was a utilitarian one emphasizing the cost of cigarette smoking in terms of premature deaths and lost working days. With the introduction of the passive smoking issue, the ethical arguments used against cigarette smoking have been greatly strengthened. The phrase "rights of the nonsmoker" has added a strong deontological argument to the already strong utilitarian arguments of the antismoking groups. Nonsmokers are claiming that the right to have clean air supersedes a smoker's right to smoke, and there are many local and state legislators who agree with this position.

Also, at the state level, the economic benefits of the cigarette industry to a non–tobacco-producing state are usually reduced to the amount of dollars the cigarette excise tax contributes to a state's coffers. All of the traditional arguments that the cigarette industry uses to justify its

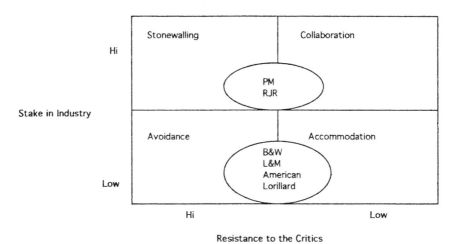

Figure 8.2 The political tactics of the big six cigarette firms. *Source:* Adapted from Post (1978), pp. 95–100.

existence lose a great deal of credibility when they are presented at the state and local level. How have the firms dealt with the seeming avalanche of adverse legislation? Figure 8.2 gives a brief graphic synopsis of the findings of Chapter 2.

It should be obvious that the political tactics employed by the individual cigarette firms are correlated to the economic stake that firm has in the industry. Philip Morris' counterattack on the antismoking movement has included publishing its own glossy general interest magazine and distributing a Great American smoker's kit, complete with ashtray guard (*New York Times Magazine*, 3/20/94, p. 34). Meanwhile, RJR, which has nearly the same market share as PM, has taken a slightly different tactic. By changing its corporate name and moving corporate headquarters, RJR seems to be willing to "accommodate" its critics. Yet RJR is still more than willing to defend its tobacco interest, and it displayed this side of its corporate character when it fired its advertising agency, Saatchi & Saatchi, after that agency had created an ad applauding Northwest Airlines' decision to ban cigarette smoking from all its flights (*Wall Street Journal*, 4/21/88, p. 12). The other four firms in the cigarette industry seem to be resigned to adverse government regulations and avoid any direct confrontations with their critics because their stake in this industry will at best be diminished in the future.

But although their critics seem to have the cigarette firms on the ropes, they face difficulties in implementing their legislative agenda.

Antismoking Groups

For antismoking groups, the arrival of the Third Wave of regulation has brought with it a period of great triumph over the cigarette industry. Although the antismoking forces such as GASP and ASH still expend most of their efforts on national legislation, they have begun to turn their attention to the state and local levels of government. One of the more interesting developments has been the way in which radical antismoking groups have been able to combine their efforts with more traditional antismoking groups such as the American Heart, Cancer, and Lung societies at the state and local level. What should alarm the cigarette industry about this merger is that the rhetoric and demands adopted by these combined forces are those originally proposed by the radical groups. The ideological consensus that was reached between the two groups was resolved in favor of the radical groups and any moderate positions toward the cigarette industry have been abandoned. For all of these groups now have as their common goal a smoke-free society by the year 2000, and with it, the total abolition of the cigarette industry. However, there is little doubt that the 1994 elections were a blow to antismoking forces, especially at the federal level. Key committees in both the House and Senate are now controlled by forces much more sympathetic to the cigarette industry. Yet, as was pointed out in Chapter 6, this election will also put additional pressure on states to raise revenue, and the cigarette excise taxes will certainly be a favorite target.

This nonconciliatory attitude toward the cigarette industry by the antismoking groups can also pose some problems for these groups. Although these groups certainly want to reinforce the antismoking ideology that has developed since 1985, they cannot afford the label of "ideologues"; antismoking groups should take pains to avoid a reputation of being latter-day Prohibitionists. Just how hard and fast the antismoking movement can push its legislative program remains to be seen. Yet these groups also have to take advantage of the momentum they have built over the past few years, especially at the state and local levels. Therefore, the problem the antismoking forces have is to find the appropriate speed to move their agenda through the various levels and branches of government without being perceived as antismoking fanatics or dissipating the tremendous antismoking sentiment that now exists in the United States. If the antismoking groups play the game correctly, they are certainly in a position to achieve their goals. However, the task will be quite complex, and the cigarette industry will prove to be a formidable foe no matter how weakened it has become by this current wave of government interventions.

LESSONS OF THE CIGARETTE INDUSTRY FOR THE FUTURE OF THE BUSINESS AND PUBLIC POLICY PROCESS

Once again, I will use the Convergence Model of Business and Public Policy to illustrate how a future issue set for other industries could be formed and the path that issue set must travel through the Business and Public Policy processes.

The unique theoretical issues that this model had to deal with to fit the cigarette industry but that are not unique to this industry were (1) the timing factor which every issue set had to possess if it hoped to be introduced into the Business and Public Policy processes; (2) the level of government intervention in Public Policy controversies; and (3) the role of ethical argumentation in the formation of an issue set. These concepts will determine how an industry and public policy will interact as they interact with one another in the Business and Public Policy processes.

"Timing" Problems for Business and Public Policy Issues

Throughout this study of the cigarette industry, we have seen how the concept "time" has been of critical importance to this study in two ways. In Chapter 2, the history of the cigarette industry was divided into three time periods or waves. Each wave represented a new round of government interventions the cigarette industry had to face. It was also determined that the issues from a previous wave were still present in succeeding waves. Although each wave was powered by a new issue (antitrust, smoking and health, passive smoking), issues from previous waves were still present. The concept of the the life cycle of an issue needs to be expanded to show how an issue set can be expanded and renewed with the passage of time. We have also seen that an issue is rarely completely settled but usually combines with additional issues as time goes along.

Second, we have also seen throughout this book how the timing of a policy intervention was of critical importance as to whether or not an intervention would succeed in achieving the goal of policy makers. Rhode Island's cigarette excise tax increase succeeded in reducing cigarette sales because it was coordinated with previous cigarette excise tax increases. The ban on TV and radio of cigarette advertising was implemented at a time that had the unintended effect of reinforcing the duopolistic tendency of the cigarette industry. This timing problem, however, cannot be confined to just the consequences of public policy interventions but also must be extended to the early parts of the Convergence Model of Business and Public Policy.

First, activists and business policy makers need to deal with the timing element necessary to publicize an issue set. How will the various media (academic journals, print, TV) have to be coordinated if activist groups are to succeed in forming or revitalizing an issue set? When should these groups take an issue national? When can they bring it to the state or local level? How do business policy makers respond to the activist's issue set agenda?

Activists and business policy makers must also answer the questions: When should they bring that issue set to the public policy process? To what branch and to what level of government should these groups bring the issue set when they decide to present their interest?

The concept of the life cycle of public issues (Post, 1978, p. 78) is one way to begin developing this concept of timing, especially with its emphasis on evolutionary change and its concern with where pressure can be applied at various times. However, the one common theme that all of these timing elements had is the level of government or the firm on which they operate.

Level(s) of Introducing an Issue Set

An interesting assumption or bias that most public policy and social issue management theorists have had in the past is the assumption that public policy issues are settled at the federal level. Admittedly, most of the major public policy issues of the 1960s and 1970s such as civil rights and Medicare were settled at the federal level. But in the 1980s and the 1990s, with the coming of the Reagan and Bush administrations, a renewed emphasis was placed on solving public policy issues at the state or local levels of government. The fact that an issue set would be of interest to some regions of the country and not to others must be acknowledged by public policy theorists. Another interesting factor that public policy analyses have often ignored is that issue sets are sometimes much more easily resolved at the state and local levels of government than at the federal level. This is especially true when a state or region has no economic interest in a particular business or industry and so that level of government has little difficulty in passing legislation regulating the activity of that business or industry. Certainly, the states that had no compunction about regulating the cigarette industry were those that had little to lose economically. Meanwhile, the tobacco-growing states passed few if any pieces of legislation regulating this industry. This observation is hardly surprising but it is also rarely acknowledged in public policy models because the role of the states in regulating business and industry is also usually ignored. Thus, there are three questions that business and public policy makers must address: (1) How does one account for the differences in the public policy process from state to state? (2) How does the federal policy process differ from the local and state public policy processes? (3) How do business policy makers react to the changes in the public policy process when an issue set is brought to the state and local levels of government?

Future business and public policy makers do have a place to start as they begin to answer these questions. The "Interpenetrating Systems Model" of Preston and Post (1975, p. 24) recognizes that a society functions by using both "macro-systems" and "micro-organizations." This model also acknowledges that these "systems" and "organizations" are dependent upon each other and cannot exist independently. One could conceive of a model in which the issue set creation process, the public policy process, and the business policy process are all systems that are not only dependent on each other but also on organizations such as activists groups, business firms, and state and local governments, which in turn are dependent on these larger systems.

Our analysis of the cigarette industry certainly points out that the concepts of timing and level are essential to anyone who wants to predict how an issue will develop. The type of approach that seems best suited to incorporating these concepts is a systems approach. Business and public policy analysts for industries such as alcohol, gambling, oil, and export industries will find this type of thinking essential. But there is still one final element that future policy makers have to include in any model of the business and public processes, and that element is the role of ethical thinking in developing an issue set.

Ethical Reasoning and the Issue Set

The cigarette industry has always been a target of public criticism, but it did not begin to lose the ethical battle over smoking until the beginning of the Third Wave of regulation and the passive smoking issue. What were the characteristics of the passive smoking issue that made it possible for antismoking groups to win the hearts and minds of the public and its public policy makers? Perhaps the easiest way of explaining this ethical value phenomenon is to compare cigarette smoking with another controversial issue, gambling. Why was cigarette smoking condemned by the majority of public policy makers whereas gambling was seemingly being promoted by many public policy makers as a painless cure to our public financing problems? I will now compare gambling and cigarette smoking as public issues to elucidate for the reader the type of ethical thinking that now dominates the American public policy process.

The current controversy over gambling as a public policy issue has a nearly thirty-year history starting with New Hampshire's adoption of a lottery in 1964. At that time, gambling was roundly condemned by most segments of U.S. society. Casino gambling was confined to Nevada, and horse and dog racing were tolerated because they were "sporting" events made possible by betting on the various races. New Hampshire had become the first state to approve a lottery in a very controversial election. Before this newly legalized state-sponsored lottery, only charitable institutions such as churches and fire companies were permitted to run bingo games and 50/50 chances in order to provide revenue for good causes. But in general, government at all levels bowed to public sentiment and discouraged gambling. It was considered an intolerable activity and therefore the "right" to gamble was easily sacrificed.

However, thirty years later, gambling has been become an acceptable recreational activity. Thirty-seven states and the District of Columbia have sponsored lotteries and other forms of gambling such as keno and video poker. In addition, the number of states that sanction some form of casino gambling is also growing rapidly. In 1993, state-sponsored gambling contributed well over $13.5 billion to government treasuries. By way of comparison, the contribution that gambling makes to government's coffers is two and half times what people spend on movie tickets in the United States.

Once again, if we return to 1964, cigarette smoking was an activity tolerated by public policy makers because the majority of the public viewed it as merely a slightly unhealthy activity. Cigarette smoking is a source of income that can be "justified" (i.e., made tolerable) by leveling excise taxes, known as "sin" taxes. Cigarette smokers considered smoking a right to which they were entitled in order to deal with the various stresses of life. If they were harming anyone, it was only themselves. Meanwhile, antismoking forces insisted that cigarette smoking ought to be discouraged if not outlawed because it was in society's best interest. However, the economic benefits from cigarette production and the rights of the cigarette smokers triumphed over the "societal good" argument. But with the coming of the passive smoking issue in 1985, the previous tolerance of cigarette smoking became a thing of the past. Smoking is rapidly being banished from all public places.

It is truly remarkable that smoking and gambling have experienced an almost complete role reversal in their places in the public policy process. A majority of the U.S. population now views cigarette smokers as pariahs who are to be banished from offices and most public places whereas gambling is now considered a legitimate form of entertainment in most sections of the United States with the exception of the southern Bible Belt.

Why has the debate over gambling and smoking evolved so differently over the course of the past thirty years? One way to account for this development is to examine the way in which the merits of a public policy issue are debated. In the United States, the conflict between the societal good and the rights of the individual has been historically the focus of the ethical controversy surrounding numerous U.S. public policy debates. Debates over controversial issues such as slavery, states' rights, and even Prohibition were constantly appealing to either of these ethical schools in making their cases either pro or con. It is still the basis for debating the ethical merits of public policy issues ranging from environmental issues to gun control. Hence, throughout U.S. history, public policy makers constantly have had to balance this conflict between the common good versus the right of the individual to choose freely. It has resulted in two competing schools of ethical thought—the "Ethics of Sacrifice" and the "Ethics of Tolerance" (McGowan, 1994).

Ethics of Sacrifice

When sacrifice is used as a moral concept to advance the merits of a particular public policy issue, public policy makers try to persuade the public that it must give up some benefit or "right" in order to achieve a noble goal or an end. This appeal can be easily invoked by religious leaders, but it can also be employed by political leaders in times of great national crisis, especially in times of popular wars such World War I or II. The "Ethics of Sacrifice" is goal or end oriented. The goal is the good of society and the goodness of any action is measured by what it contributes to maintaining the good of society.

In terms of public policy, the "good end" is a harmonious society. Traditionally, this ethic has been invoked by those who want to maintain social institutions and structures they deem desirable and to be maintained at any cost. Witness the concern of public policy makers over maintaining "family values." Although some might associate this type of ethical reasoning with "conservative" policy makers, it has actually been used by both conservative and liberal thinkers to justify their stance on major public policy issues. Liberal politicians such as John F. Kennedy certainly invoked the "Ethics of Sacrifice" with his famous phrase: "Ask not what your country can do for you; ask what you can do for your country!" In essence, those who utilize the "Ethics of Sacrifice" are asking the public to subordinate what is good for the individual to what is good for all.

An example of how institutions influence our understanding of the common good was written by A. Bartlett Giamatti, the recently deceased commissioner of baseball, on the occasion of his decision to ban Pete Rose from baseball. Giamatti stated:

> I believe that baseball is a beautiful and exciting game, loved by millions— I among them—and I believe that baseball is an important, enduring American institution. It must assert and aspire to the highest of principles—of integrity, of professionalism of performance, of fair play within its rules. It will come as no surprise that like any institution composed of human beings, this institution will not always fulfill its highest aspirations. I know of no earthly institution that does. But this one, because it is so much a part of our history as a people and because it has such a purchase on our national soul, has an obligation to the people for whom it is played—to its fans and its well-wishers—to strive for excellence in all things and to promote the highest ideal. (*The New York Times,* August 11, 1989, section 1, p. 23)

The advocates of the "Ethics of Sacrifice" equate the preservation of institutions with the maintenance of the good life. Pete Rose's decision to gamble had to be punished severely because his gambling had damaged an institution that inspires people to act virtuously. The decision as to whether an individual has the right to perform certain actions has to be measure in terms of what effect an action will have on an institution. Because Rose damaged this noble institution, he had to be banished from it.

Ethics of Tolerance

One of the earliest virtues which every American schoolchild is taught is tolerance. To escape religious persecution in England, the Quakers settled in Pennsylvania and are celebrated in American history texts because they permitted everyone to practice their religious beliefs. In founding Maryland, Lord Baltimore also established freedom of religion, especially for persecuted English Catholics, although this religious tolerance would be tested frequently throughout the colonial period. The Pilgrims who settled Massachusetts were also trying to escape religious persecution; however, tolerance was not a Puritan virtue, as Roger Williams, the founder of Rhode Island, quickly found out when he was forced to flee Massachusetts. Although there have been difficulties throughout U.S. history, tolerance for different religions and different nationalities has been one of the hallmarks of American society in comparison to most societies.

Tolerance entails that no person has to sacrifice her or his basic freedoms in order to achieve some goal of public welfare or to preserve some institution. Society cannot countenance the abandonment of any individual even if society must incur a heavy cost to save that individual from activities deemed harmful to that individual. It also entails that American society has to tolerate the right of the individual to perform actions that might very well be destructive to that society, as long as the right to perform those activities is guaranteed by law.

A recent example of where the "Ethics of Tolerance" has so far prevailed in the public policy forum is the gun control issue. Opponents of gun control have used the "Ethics of Tolerance" as the basis of their moral public policy argument. They maintain that the right to bear arms has to be tolerated even if the majority of the nation wishes to put some limits on this right. Society has to tolerate the possible improper use of guns in order to uphold the rights of a minority who wish to have no limits on their ability to own guns.

The "Ethics of Tolerance" is based on a noble American value and experiment: we must never use a citizen as a means to achieve an end. Government exists to protect the individual's rights and must not coerce an individual to relinquish a "right," even to preserve an institution that has served society well. It is a value that in many ways is a necessity in a country of immigrants. These immigrants had to be tolerated and protected to promote diversity in a society.

The Triumph of the Ethics of Tolerance

Advocates of either legalizing lotteries (or other types of gambling activities) or reducing government involvement in the cigarette industry invariably employ the "Ethics of Tolerance" as their primary moral argument when approaching the public policy arena. Their argument for both issues is simply that society must tolerate these activities because individuals should have the right to engage in them as long as they are not harming anyone else. These advocates also attempt to counter the "Ethics of Sacrifice" by noting the potential economic contributions of these "sin industries." They acknowledge that these activities might be harmful to some individuals, but insist that the state or charities ought to be able to profit from these activities because most smokers or gamblers will continue to smoke or gamble whether or not the state permits these activities. So why shouldn't the state or a charity use the profit from them for a "good" cause?

Meanwhile, opponents of these two "sinful" activities have generally employ the "Ethics of Sacrifice" as their primary ethical resource in their fights against these vices. They would argue that any benefits that accrue to society by allowing these activities in no way justifies them. Society must protect itself from activities that bring great harm on various segments of society. The harm done to society at large more than outweighs the harm done by violating an individual's right to engage in these activities. Therefore, government ought to "sacrifice" lotteries (or other types of gambling) and the rights of cigarette smokers for society's overall good.

The recent surge in establishing state lotteries and other forms of state-sponsored gambling indicates that public policy makers sense that the majority of their constituencies are in agreement with the tenets of the "Ethics of Tolerance" in regard to the gambling issue. Indeed, when it comes to the lottery and gambling issue, it appears that the public is *not* willing to sacrifice the right to gamble or the income that comes from state-sponsored gambling.

Antismoking forces have achieved their greatest success when they were finally able to employ the "Ethics of Tolerance" to make their cases for enacting antismoking ordinances in public places. Using the passive smoking issue along with their traditional "common good" arguments, antismoking activists now argue that cigarette smoking does indeed harm the nonsmoker and therefore the smoker's right to smoke has to be limited to those occasions where the smoker is only harming herself or himself.

Implications of the Triumph of the "Ethics of Tolerance"

In trying to understand why two public policy issues such as lotteries (gambling) and smoking have evolved so differently over the past thirty years, the conclusion reached was that there has been a change in the basic ethic that motivates public policy makers. It represents the triumph of the rights of individuals ("Ethics of Tolerance") over the good of societal institutions ("Ethics of Sacrifice"). With the triumph of the "Ethics of Tolerance," it appears that the new categorical imperative that public policy makers operate under is this: "You have the right to perform any action as long that action does not interfere with the rights of others."

This triumph of the "Ethics of Tolerance" does not preclude the "Ethics of Sacrifice" from playing a significant role in the current public policy process; the "Ethics of Sacrifice" might "triumph" again in the future. But this triumph of the "Ethics of Tolerance" does indicate that, at least for the foreseeable future, most public policy issues will be settled in favor of those who can employ the arguments generated from the "Ethics of Tolerance."

During the past thirty years, tolerance has become the highest civic virtue because it makes living in a pluralistic society possible. No doubt, we have witnessed societies such as the former USSR, China, Cuba, and Iran where there is no tolerance for diversity. The preceding examples of conformist societies have convinced Americans that they certainly want to avoid this type of conformist ethic. It was in reaction to this conformist ethic that the "Ethics of Tolerance" was formulated. We should tolerate any action by an individual as long as that action enables that individual to be true to one's self and doesn't violate the rights of another individual. This ethical principle represents the triumph of the self over all other moral considerations. Nor is this self the one advocated by Kant, which was conceived as having to obey univerisal "Practical Reasoning." Rather, the self that the "Ethics of Tolerance" promotes is the temporary self where long-term consequences are ignored so that the individual retains his or her autonomy. Just as American businesspersons have been criticized for focusing too much on short-term financial goals, it appears that U.S. public policy makers have also fallen into this trap of short-termism. This adoption of the "Ethics of Tolerance," with its focus of tolerating activities in order to maintain the short-term peace, will have very interesting consequences for the type of society that the United States will be for the foreseeable future.

The continuing support public policy makers give to "tolerance" merely confirms the present U.S. cultural tendency to withdraw from public action into a cocoon of privacy. This preoccupation with the self or privacy poses some real challenges to the whole system of values and obligations that have historically been the basis of community and our cherished institutions such as the family. Permitting people to be "free" to do what they want as long as they do not hurt others is hardly the type of ethic needed when American society seems to be so desperately in need of a unifying communitarian spirit. Needless to say, this is not a call to subjugate the self or individual freedom totally under the banner of communitarian or institutional need. But certainly this study of the problems of the tobacco industry in the United States points out a real need for American society to develop an ethic supporting a series of objective norms that can be used to referee between the legitimate needs of society's institutions and the yearnings of the self.

What this study of the cigarette industry points out is the need to restore a balance between the concerns of those who support the "Ethics of Tolerance" with those who support the "Ethics of Sacrifice" when the public policy process is trying to deal with an issue that has ethical implications.

CONCLUSION

The problems that business and public policy makers face as they examine the cigarette industry are in no way unique. The timing, level, and ethical components of the Convergence Model are present in every industry that has a stake in the business and public policy processes. We have seen how the policy interventions that have been imposed upon the cigarette industry have changed both the strategies of the firms and the structure of that industry. No doubt, the same type of intended and unintended changes will occur in other industries (ranging from alcohol to shoes!) facing similar governmental actions.

The business strategies of the cigarette industry and the public policy issues surrounding this controversial industry have been in many ways prophetic. The tobacco industry was one of the first industries to diversify on a corporate level and segment its product on a business level. Many corporations have tried to emulate the cigarette industry's corporate and business strategies because the cigarette industry showed how these strategies could be employed successfully. The cigarette industry's relationship to government has also been instructive to other industries. Its relationship to the judicial, legislative, and executive branches of government were a forerunner for similar types of relationships for other industries such as alcohol, oil, drugs, and others.

There is little doubt that the cigarette industry will face additional demands from the American public in the future after a brief respite in the late 1990s. With the advent of a Republican Congress in 1995, the industry will no doubt weather any potential legislative storms. However, antismoking activists will once again return to the judicial branch as they continue their attack on the tobacco industry (*Boston Globe*, 12/14/94, p. 3). The industry will no doubt tie up these legal challenges in court, but suits brought by antismoking activists will keep the smoking and health issue alive and well on the public policy agenda. There is little doubt that a Fourth Wave of regulation will result. What issue will send this new wave into motion is hard to predict, but because none of the current controversies surrounding the cigarette industry have been settled, whatever this new issue is, it will join forces with the issues of the three previous waves to force the cigarette industry once again to justify its existence to public policy makers.

As the cigarette industry faces its future, its international nature will be its greatest threat as well as opportunity. Once again, the cigarette industry will encounter problems much sooner on this international frontier than its counterparts in other industries. How the cigarette industry will deal with the problems of revenue and smoking and health in the international context has yet to be determined. If the cigarette industry fails to deal with these problems, its future appears to be dim. But it has managed to survive before, and foreign governments seem to tolerate cigarette smoking as a lucrative source of revenue.

As this controversial industry moves into the twenty-first century, it is a reminder that the twentieth century has been one in which both business and public policy makers have been fixated on short-term rather than long-term consequences of their actions. Cigarette smoking has given many individuals short-term pleasure at a potentially deadly long-term cost. But what is true for individuals is also quite pertinent for society in general. Although the revenue from cigarette excise taxes enables public policy makers to balance budgets in the short run, the cigarette excise tax cannot be and was never meant to be—a long-term solution to financing needed government services. As these same policy makers move into the twenty-first century, they will perhaps realize the necessity of taking into account the long-term implications of their actions.

Bibliography

American Brands. *Annual Reports, 10K reports,* 1965 to 1994.

Bass, F.M. "A Simultaneous Equation Regression Study of Advertising and Sales of Cigarettes," *Journal of Marketing Research* (August 1969) 6: 291–300.

Berger, Peter. "A Sociological View of the Antismoking Phenomenon," in Tollison: *Smoking and Society,* Lexington, Mass.: Lexington Books, pp. 225–240.

Biggadike, E.R. *Corporate Diversification: Entry, Strategy, and Performance.* Boston: Division of Research, Graduate School of Business Administration, Harvard University, 1976.

———"The Risky Business of Diversification," *Harvard Business Review,* (May–June 1979): 103–111.

Boston Globe. Kenen, J. "Foes of Smoking Hit Tobacco Firms' Ads," July 27, 1994, p. 3.

———Hobler, R. "Alleging Tobacco Conspiracy, Mehan to Urge US Grand Jury Inquiry," December 14, 1994, p. 3.

Boston Herald. "RJR Plans to Retire Debt," November 1, 1994, p. 33.

Box, G.E.P. and G.M. Jenkins. *Time Series Analysis: Forecasting and Control.* San Francisco: Holden-Day, 1976.

Box, G.E.P. and G.C. Tiao. "Intervention Analysis with Applications to Economic and Environmental Problems," *Journal of the American Statistical Association* (March 1975)70 (349) :70–79.

Business Week. Annual Survey of the Cigarette Industry, 1947–1994.

———"The Concentration of the Cigarette Industry," January 18, 1985, p. 90.

———"Nonfiltered Has Taken Over the Cigarette Market," December 26, 1986, p. 66.

———"Miller Continues to Lose to Bud," February 1, 1988, p. 26.

———"Secondhand Smoke at RJR Nabisco," May 3, 1993, pp. 130–132.

———"RJR and KKK: Round Two," August 30, 1993, p. 58.

———"Are Cigarette Firms Charging Too Much?" February 2, 1994, p. 21.

————"Turning the Tables: Foreign Tobacco Turns Towards US," May 16, 1994, p. 126.

————"Tobacco: Does It Have a Future?" July 4, 1994, pp. 24–29.

Calirmonte, F. "The Transnational Tobacco and Alcohol Conglomerates: A World Oligopoly," *NY Journal of Medicine* (1993) 83:1322–1344.

Campbell, D. and J. Stanley. *Experimental and Quasi-Experimental Design for Research.* Chicago: Rand-McNally Co., 1963.

Carroll, A. *Business and Society: Managing Corporate Social Performance.* Boston: Little Brown, 1993.

Castaneda, J. *El Consumo de Tabaco en Espana y sus Factores.* Edicion Homenaie de Tabacalera, S.A. Madrid: Tabapress, S.A. 1988.

Chappell, V.G. "The Economic Effect of Excise Taxes on Tobacco Products," *Tobacco International* (August 1984) 186(16):14–16.

Congressional Budget Office, "Cigarette Excise Taxes and Sales," January 1985.

————"The Tobacco Industry," Spring 1987.

————"Excise Taxes and Budgetary Controls," June 1993.

————"Passive Smoking as an Issue," April 14, 1994.

Coultas, D.B. and J.M. Samet. "Passive Smoking and Health," *Western Journal of Medicine* (March 1986) 144(3):350–355.

Cox, R. *Competition in the American Tobacco Industry: 1911–1932.* New York: Columbia University Press, 1933.

Department of Health and Human Services. *The Health Consequences of Smoking: Cancer, A Report of the Surgeon General.* Rockville, Md. 1982.

Department of Health and Human Services. *The Health Consequences of Smoking: Cardiovascular Disease, A Report of the Surgeon General.* Rockville, Md. 1983.

Department of Health and Human Services. *The Health Consequences of Smoking: Chronic Obstructive Lung Disease, A Report of the Surgeon General.* Rockville, Md. 1984.

Department of Health and Human Services. *The Health Consequences of Smoking for Women, A Report of the Surgeon General.* Rockville, Md. 1980.

Doron, G. *The Smoking Paradox: Public Regulation in the Cigarette Industry.* Cambridge, Mass.: Abt Books, 1979.

Dye, T. *Understanding Public Policy,* 3rd. ed. Englewood Cliffs, N.J.: Prentice-Hall, 1978.

The Economist."Smoking 'em Out," September 15, 1990, 83.

————"BAT Buys American," April 30, 1994, 75.

————"Still Smokin'," March 11, 1995, 61.

Edelmann, M. *The Symbolic Uses of Politics.* Urbana, Ill.: University of Illinois Press, 1964.

Eleazer, T. "Planning Diversification at RJR," *Bottom Line.* Chapel Hill, N.C.: Graduate School of Business Administration, University of North Carolina (December 1977).

Fahey, L. and V.K. Narayanan. *Macroeconomic Analysis for Strategic Management* St. Paul, Minn.: West Publishing, 1986.

Finger,W.R., ed. *The Tobacco Industry in Transition.* Lexington, Mass.: Lexington Books, 1981.

Fortune."The Tobacco Lobby," August 17, 1987: 71.

———"RJR's New Image," July 18, 1988, 37.

———"Synar Goes after Tobacco Again," August 24, 1994, 74.

Freeman, R.E. *Strategic Management: A Stakeholder Approach,* Boston: Pitman Books, 1984.

Friedman, K.M. *Public Policy and the Smoking-Health Controversy.* Lexington, Mass.: Lexington Books, 1975.

Fritschler, A.L. *Smoking and Politics: Policymaking and the Federal Bureaucracy.* 2nd ed., Englewood Cliffs, N.J.: Prentice-Hall, 1975.

Fujii, E.T. "The Demand for Cigarettes: Further Empirical Evidence and Its Implications for Public Policy," *Applied Economics* (December 1980) 12:479–489.

GASP. "Newsletter," January 1992.

Hamilton, J.L. "The Demand for Cigarettes: Advertising, Health Scare and the Advertising Ban," *Review of Economics and Statistics* (1972) 54:401–411.

Harris, J. E. "On the Fairness of Cigarette Excise Taxation," Proceedings of the Conference on the Cigarette Excise Tax, *Institute for the Study of Smoking Behavior,* Harvard University, 1987, pp. 106–111.

Hirayama, T. "Cancer Mortality in Nonsmoking Women with Smoking Husbands Based on a Large Scale Cohort Study in Japan," *Preventive Medicine* (1985) 13:680–690.

Jacobstein, M. *The Tobacco Industry in the U.S.* 1st ed. New York: Columbia University Press, 1908.

Johnson, P.R. *The Economics of the Tobacco Industry.* New York: Praeger Publishers, 1984.

Leontiades, M. *Strategies for Diversification and Change.* Boston: Little, Brown, 1980.

Lexis, "Corporate Summaries," Ligget Group, 1985.

Ligget Group, Inc. *Annual Reports and 10K Reports,* 1960–1994.

Lindblom, C.E. "The Science of 'Muddling Through,'" *Public Administrative Review* (Spring 1959):79–88.

Ljung, G.M. and G.E.P. Box. "On a Measure of Lack of Fit in Time Series Models," *Biometrika* (August 1978) 65(2): 297–303.

Lodge, G. "The Large Corporation and the New American Ideology," in *Corporations and the Common Good,* Dickie, R. and L. Rouner, ed. Notre Dame, Ind.: Notre Dame Press, 1986, pp. 61–77.

Lorillard, Inc. *Annual Reports and 10K Reports,* 1965–1994.

Loews, Inc. *Annual Reports and 10K Reports,* 1969–1994.

Lyon, H.L. and J.L. Simon. "Price Elasticity of Demand for Cigarettes in the United States," *American Journal of Agricultural Economics* (1968) 50(4):88–95.

Mahon J. "Corporate Political Strategies: An Empirical Study of Chemical Firms Responses to Surperfund Legislation," *Research in Corporate Social Performance and Policy,* ed. L. Preston. Greenwich, Conn.: JAI Press, 1983.

Markham, J.W. *Conglomerate Enterprise and Public Policy.* Boston: Division of Research, Graduate School of Business Administration, Harvard University, 1973.

McCleary, R. and R.A. Hay Jr. *Applied Time Series Analysis for the Social Sciences.* Beverly Hills, Calif.: Sage Publications, 1980.

McGowan, R.A. "Public Policy Measures and Cigarette Sales: An ARIMA Intervention Analysis," in *Research in Corporate Social Performance and Policy*, ed. James Post. Greenwich, Conn.: JAI Press, 1989.

——*State Lotteries and Legalized Gambling*. Westport, Conn.: Praeger, 1994.

Memoria Tabacalera, S.A., Tabapress, S.A., published annual reports since 1978.

Miles, R. *Coffin Nails and Corporate Strategies*. Englewood Cliffs, N.J.: Prentice-Hall, 1982.

Miller, R.H. "Factors Affecting Cigarette Consumption," paper presented at the *National Tobacco Tax Association Annual Meeting*, Kiamesha, N.Y. (September 1974).

Neuberger, M. B. *Smoke Screen: Tobacco and the Public Welfare*. Englewood Cliffs, N.J.: Prentice-Hall, 1963.

New York Times. Harris, J. "Break up the Cigarette Cartel," January 30, 1987, p. 57.

——Van Gelder, L. "New Troubles for the Tobacco Industry," June 14, 1988, p. D. 1.

——Gray, J. "Wages of Sin Down and That's Hurting State Tax Revenues," March 2, 1993, p. A1.

——Smothers, R. "Tobacco Country Is Quaking over Cigarette Tax Proposal," March 22, 1993, p. A2.

——Elliot, S. "A Showdown for Marlboro," April 6, 1993, p. D1.

——Sterngold, J. "When Smoking Is a Patriotic Duty," October 17, 1993, Section 3, p. 1.

——Janofsky, M. "On Cigarettes, Health and Lawyers," December 6, 1993, p. D1.

——Eaton, L. "Who Wants Philip Morris with Its Problems? Many Investors Do," June 24, 1994, p. D8.

——Collins, G. "Borden Agrees to Takeover," September 13, 1994, p. D1.

——Elliot, S. "Justice to Block Tobacco Merger," November 2, 1994, p. D1.

——Elliot, S. "R.J. Reynolds Tobacco Renews Its Hope That Where There's Low Smoke, There's Marketing Fire," November 29, 1994, p. D20.

New York Times Magazine. Rosenblatt, R. "How Do They Live with Themselves?" March 20, 1994.

Nichlaides-Bouman, A. and et al., *International Smoking Statistics*. London: Oxford University Press, 1993.

Nicholls, W.H. *Price Policies in the Cigarette Industry*. Nashville, TN: Vanderbilt University Press, 1951.

Office of Technology Assessment, U.S. Congress, Staff Paper. *Passive Smoking in the Workplace: Selected Issues* (May, 1994): 19–22.

Philadelphia Inquirer. Brink, B.F. "The Cigarette Population," July 2, 1990, p. 2.

Philip Morris, Inc. *Annual Reports and 10K Reports*, 1960–1994.

Pint, Ellen M. "Nationalization and Privatization," *Journal of Public Policy* (1990) 10:263–273.

Pitts, R.A. "Diversification Strategies and Organizational Policies of Large Diversified Firms," *Journal of Economics and Business*, 28 (Spring-Summer 1979): 181–188.

Porter, M. *Competitive Strategy: Techniques for Analyzing Industries and Competitors*. New York: Free Press, 1980.

Post, J. *Corporate Behavior and Social Change*, Reston,VA.: Reston Publishing, 1978.

Preston, L. and Post, J. *Private Management and Public Policy*, Englewood Cliffs, N.J.: Prentice-Hall, 1975.

RJR Industries. *Annual Reports and 10 K Reports*, 1965–1985.

RJR Nabisco. *Annual Report and 10 K Report*, 1986–1994.

Robert, J. C. *The Story of Tobacco in America*. Chapel Hill: University of North Carolina, 1967.

Sapolsky, H.M. " The Political Obstacles to the Control of Cigarette Smoking in the United States" *Journal of Health Politics and Law* (Summer 1980) 5(2):277–290.

Schmalense, R. L. *The Economics of Advertising*. Amsterdam: North Holland Publishing Co., 1972.

Sullivan, D. A. "Testing Hypotheses about Firm Behavior in the Cigarette Industry," *Journal of Political Economy*, (1985) 93:586–598.

Sumner, D. A., and M. K. Wohlgenant. "Effects of an Increase in the Federal Excise Tax on Cigarettes," *American Journal of Agricultural Economics* (May 1985) 67:235–242.

Sumner, M. and R. Ward. "Tax Change and Cigarette Prices," *Journal of Political Economy* (December 1981) 89:1261–1265.

A Report of the Surgeon General: The Health Consequences of Smoking, Department of Health and Human Services, Rockville, Md. 1985.

A Report of the Surgeon General: The Health Consequences of Smoking, Department of Health and Human Services, Rockville, Md. 1986.

A Report of the Surgeon General: The Health Consequences of Smoking, Department of Health and Human Services, Rockville, Md. 1988.

Taylor, S. "Tobacco and Economic Growth in Developing Countries," *Business in the Contemporary World*, Winter 1989.

Tennant, R. *The American Cigarette Industry*. New Haven, Conn: Yale University Press, 1950.

Tilley, N.M. *R.J. Reynolds: Our 100th Anniversary (1875–1975)* Winston-Salem, N.C.: 1975.

Time. "Tobacco's Diversification," January 18, 1985, p. 71.

———"Liability and Tobacco," June 27, 1988, p. 48.

The Tobacco Institute. *Facts About Cigarettes*, 1993.

———*The Economic Impact of Tobacco on the U.S. Economy*, 1983–1994.

———*The Excise Tax: Fairness Issue*, 1984–1994.

———*Tobacco Industry Profile, 1985–1994*. Washington, D.C., published yearly since 1985.

———*Smoking Restrictions*, (1986, 1994) Washington, D.C. A summary of various state's smoking restrictions laws.

———*Tobacco Smoke and the Nonsmoker: Scientific Integrity at the Crossroads*, Washington, D.C., 1994.

Tobacco International. "WHO Survey Reveals More Youths, Especially Girls are Smoking." New York (1982) 184(16):10, 12, 13.

The Tobacco Observer, published by the Tobacco Institute, is a summary of the various activities and new releases that this group sponsors. It has been published quarterly since 1965.

Tobacco Tax Council, Inc. *The Tax Burden on Tobacco: Historical Compilation, Vol. 29.* Richmond, Va. : (1994) Tobacco Institute Publication.

Tollison, Robert D. *Smoking and Society.* Lexington, Mass.: Lexington Books, 1986.

———*Clearing the Air: Perspectives on Environmental Tobacco Smoke.* Lexington, Mass.: Lexington Books, 1988.

———and R. E. Wagner. *Smoking and the State.* Lexington, Mass.: Lexington Books, 1988.

Troyer, M. and B. Markle, *Cooperative Lobbying: The Power of Pressure.* Tucson, University of Arizona Press, 1986.

Tye, J. *Newsletter of STAT* (Stop Teenage Abuse of Tobacco), 1986–1993.

U.S. Department of Health, Education and Welfare. *Smoking and Health: Report of the Advisory Committee to the Surgeon General of the Public Health Service.* Washington: U.S. Government Printing Office, 1964. This report is often referred to as the Surgeon General's Report.

U.S. Department of Health, Education and Welfare. *Smoking and Health: A Report of the Surgeon General.* Washington, D.C. (1979–1980).

Vickers, John and George Yarrow. *Privatization: An Economic Analysis.* Cambridge, Mass: MIT Press, 1988.

Wall Street Journal. Staff, "PM Purchase of GF Completed," September 30, 1985, p. 2.

———Hevesi, D. "RJR Moves to Atlanta," January 12, 1987, p. 37.

———Belluck, P. "Cipollone Case Strikes the Tobacco Industry," June 4, 1988, p. 1.

———Becker, G. S. and M.Grossman. "Cigarette Revenue Up in Smoke, " August 9, 1994, p. A12.

Warner, K.E. "Cigarette Taxation: Doing Good by Doing Well," *Journal of Public Health* (September 1980) 5(3):312–319.

———"Smoking and Health Implications of a Change in the Federal Excise Tax," *Journal of the American Medical Association* (February 28, 1985) 255:1028–1032.

———"State Legislatures on Smoking and Health: A Comparison of Two Policies," *Policy Sciences* (1991) 13:139–152.

———"Regional Differences in State Legislation on Cigarette Smoking," *Texas Business Review,* (January and February 1992) 56(1):27–29.

Whidden, P. "Effects of Passive Smoking" *Lancet* (January 1986) 8473:150.

Wilson, J. Q. "The Politics of Regulation," in James McKie (ed.), *Social Responsibility and the Business Predicament.* Washington, D.C.: Brookings Institute, 1974, pp. 155–168.

Woods, Donna. *Strategic Uses of Public Policy: Business and Government in the Progressive Era.* Marshfield, Mass.: Pitman Books, 1986.

World Health Organization. "The Effects of Advertising Bans on Cigarettes Sales," U.N. Publications, 1982.

Index

About the Author

RICHARD McGOWAN is Assistant Provost for Academic Affairs, University of Scranton. Previously he taught policy courses at Boston College's Carroll School of Management. His viewpoints on legalized gambling have made him a frequent guest on radio talkshows, including NPR's Marketplace, and in interviews with the press. The primary focus of his research is the interaction between the business and the public policy processes, especially related to tobacco, alcohol, textile, and steel industries.

ISBN 0-89930-964-X

HARDCOVER BAR CODE